Helpful Essential Links to Palliative Care

Produced and developed in the Centre for Medical Education, Ninewells Hospital and Medical School, University of Dundee, Scotland, in collaboration with Cancer Relief Macmillan Fund.

The Authors

Dr A M A Abdel-Fattah
Dr T F Benton
Ms K Copp
Dr R C Corcoran
Dr J M Leiper
Dr R H MacDougall

Mrs G Oliver
Dr W M O'Neill
Mrs F Sheldon
Mrs S Skidmore
Mr N Smith
Miss M L Thomas

Cancer Relief Advisory Group

Dr T F Benton
Ms K Copp
Dr R C Corcoran
Mr W R Dunn
Dr C Dyer
Professor G W Hanks
Professor R M Harden
Dr R Hillier
Miss J M   Laidlaw

Dr J M Leiper
Dr R H MacDougall
Mrs G Oliver
Mr W M O'Neill
Dr J Parkinson
Dr J Raiman
Mrs F Sheldon
Mrs S Skidmore

Production Team

Dr A M A Abdel-Fattah
Professor R M Harden

Miss J M Laidlaw
Miss M L Thomas.

Typing

Mrs F Johnston.

Desktop Publishing

Mrs E Jeffrey.

© 1992
ISBN No. 1 871 74926 3
Printed in Singapore

Published by the Centre for Medical Education, University of Dundee, in conjunction with Perspective, London.

Programme Development

Preliminary research into the needs of junior house officers, and other hospital staff, in palliative care was carried out. This involved extensive interviews and questionnaires.

The production team would like to thank all those who contributed to the work. Thanks also go to individuals and organisations who granted permission to reproduce some of the figures in the book and to Mr T Scott, Adviser, Cancer Relief Macmillan Fund, Edinburgh, for advice on the reading list.

Contributors

Dr A M A Abdel-Fattah
Macmillan Lecturer in Medical Education, Centre for Medical Education, Ninewells Hospital and Medical School, University of Dundee.

Dr T F Benton
Consultant, St Columba's Hospice, Edinburgh.

Ms K Copp
Macmillan Nurse Teacher, Grampian Health Board.

Dr R C Corcoran
Medical Director/Consultant, Hayward House, City Hospital, Nottingham.

Mr W R Dunn
Senior Lecturer, Department of Education, University of Glasgow.

Dr C Dyer
General Practitioner, Bonnybridge Health Centre, Bonnybridge, Scotland.

Professor G W Hanks
Sainsbury Professor of Palliative Medicine, United Medical and Dental Schools of Guy's and St Thomas's Hospitals, University of London.

Professor R M Harden
Director, Centre for Medical Education, Ninewells Hospital and Medical School, University of Dundee.

Dr R Hillier
Consultant, Countess Mountbatten House, Moorgreen Hospital, Southampton.

Miss J M Laidlaw
Co-ordinator of Postgraduate Medical and Dental Education, Postgraduate Office, Ninewells Hospital and Medical School, University of Dundee.

Dr J M Leiper
Consultant, Roxburghe House, Royal Victoria Hospital, Dundee.

Dr R H MacDougall
Clinical Director/Consultant Radiotherapist and Oncologist, Department of Clinical Oncology, Western General Hospital, Edinburgh.

Mrs G Oliver
Regional Cancer Nurse Manager, Merseyside.

Dr W M O'Neill
Senior Lecturer in Palliative Medicine, United Medical and Dental Schools of Guy's and St Thomas's Hospitals, University of London.

Dr J Parkinson
Perspective, London.

Dr J Raiman
Medical Programme Advisor, Cancer Relief Macmillan Fund.

Mrs F Sheldon
Macmillan Lecturer in Psychosocial Palliative Care, Department of Social Work Studies, University of Southampton.

Mrs S Skidmore
Macmillan Tutor, Mid-Trent College, Nottingham.

Mr N Smith
Principal Social Worker, Royal Marsden Hospital, London.

Miss M L Thomas
Macmillan Research Officer, Centre for Medical Education, Ninewells Hospital and Medical School, University of Dundee.

Foreword

"Palliative care is the active total care of patients whose disease is not responsive to curative treatment. Control of pain, of other symptoms, and of psychological, social and spiritual problems is paramount."

These words, taken from the first newsletter of the European Association for Palliative Care, encapsulate what this book is about. The development of palliative care in the past 25 years reflects a major change in attitude towards the management of patients with incurable or terminal disease. Its essence is whole patient care, family care and quality of life, based on a multidisciplinary team approach.

Considerable expertise has been built up within palliative care services. This expertise relates not just to pain and symptom control, psychological and social care but also to team working and support. The authors of this book have tried to distill some of this knowledge and convey it in a way that is relevant to everyday clinical situations. This book is designed for hospital staff, junior hospital doctors in particular, but will be relevant and useful to *anyone* directly involved in the care of patients with progressive, incurable or terminal disease.

The principles of palliative care need to be known by all those with responsibility for the care of dying patients, but are also applicable to a much wider population of patients. Little if any time is given to these matters in medical teaching, though this is a situation that is changing fast. This book is aimed at those who need to know but haven't had the opportunity to learn. I am sure that they will find it useful and that the patients and families for whom they care will benefit.

Professor Geoffrey W Hanks
Sainsbury Professor of Palliative Medicine, United Medical and Dental Schools of Guy's and St Thomas's Hospitals, University of London.

Cancer Relief Macmillan Fund

Cancer Relief Macmillan Fund is a national charity exclusively concerned with cancer care. Founded in 1911, its aim is to help improve the quality of life for people with cancer and their families, at any stage of their illness and in any setting. It achieves this through a wide range of services.

Cancer Relief Macmillan Fund provides funding for Macmillan nurses, of which there are over 950 in the UK today. Through its medical programme CRMF is also establishing a wide range of clinical consultant, senior lecturer, general practitioner facilitator and training posts in palliative medicine to assist in the development of integrated hospital and community based services. CRMF builds in-patient and day care units, provides grants for people in financial need and funds associated self-help charities. At all times CRMF works closely with the National Health Service. CRMF also funds an education programme, supporting medical and other health care professionals in developing their skills in cancer care, and has established the first United Kingdom Diploma in Palliative Medicine at the University of Wales College of Medicine.

This resource text HELP - Helpful Essential Links to Palliative Care is one of a series of educational programmes, under the name MACPAC (Macmillan Palliation and Cancer) that CRMF have developed in conjunction with the Centre for Medical Education in Dundee and the Department of Education at the University of Glasgow.

In addition to this text, a computing programme for hospital doctors is available based on a series of patient management challenges in palliative care.

Other programmes in the MACPAC series include one for general practitioners, as well as a new computing challenge for the primary health care team and an interactive video.

If you would like more information on any of these programmes please contact:
MACPAC, Centre for Medical Education, Ninewells Hospital & Medical School, Dundee DD1 9SY Scotland.
Tel:0382 60111 ex 3041.

Living with cancer

Content of Programme - Principal Sections

Section A: Pain

		Page
A1 - A6	Assessing Pain	11 - 33
A7 - A17	Particular Pain Problems	34 - 72
A18 - A20	Continuous Subcutaneous Infusion and Syringe Drivers	73 - 87
A21 - A23	Pain and the Team	88 - 94

Section B: Communication

B1 - B4	When You Need to Break Bad News	97 - 125
B5 - B9	When You are Asked Difficult Questions	126 - 143
B10 - B15	Feelings and Relationships with the Patient	144 - 165
B16 - B23	Communication with Relatives	166 - 197
B24 - B28	Communication around Death	198 - 218

Section C: Distressing Symptoms

		Page
C1 - C10	Gastro-intestinal Problems	221 - 254
C10 - C23	Other Problems	255 - 302

Section D: Context of Care

D1 - D4	Patient's Needs	305 - 317
D5 - D8	Ward Environment	318 - 327
D9 - D12	Going Home and Transfer	328 - 340

Reading list

References

Index

Contents of Programme - Problems Covered

Section A: Pain

Assessing Pain

A1   Assessing a patient's pain.
A2   The patient's subjective experience of pain.
A3   The patient has more than one pain.
A4   The patient refuses analgesia when in severe pain.
A5   You are being called repeatedly to reassess the patient's pain.
A6   The patient's pain is out of control.

Particular Pain Problems

A7   A new pain develops while the patient is on high doses of opioids.
A8   The patient has bone pain.
A9   The patient has nerve damage pain (deafferentation pain).
A10   The patient on high doses of opioids is still in pain.
A11   The patient is 'flattened' with morphine.
A12   The patient wants to be alert, not sedated.
A13   The patient refuses more treatment.
A14   A different 'starting point' for opioid in elderly patients?
A15   The patient has pain on movement.
A16   The pain relief clinic and difficult pain problems.
A17   Epidural management of pain in advanced cancer.

Continuous Subcutaneous Infusion and Syringe Drivers

A18   The most appropriate use of syringe drivers.
A19   Mixing drugs in a syringe driver.
A20   Discontinuing a subcutaneous infusion.

Pain and the Team

A21   Your senior does not appreciate that the patient is in pain.
A22   The ward team does not believe in using high doses of opioids.
A23   Colleagues feel you are overstating the patient's pain.

Section B: Communication

When You Need to Break Bad News

B1   You need to tell a patient that he or she has cancer.
B2   You need to explain to a patient that the tumour is no longer responding to treatment or that metastases have recurred.
B3   A senior team member does not think the patient should be told he or she has advanced disease.
B4   You need to break bad news over the phone.

When You are Asked Difficult Questions

B5   The patient does not want the family to know how ill he or she is.

B6   Relatives do not want the patient to know about his or her disease.

B7   The patient asks you why the treatment is not working.

B8   The patient asks you "Do you think I'll get home?"

B9   The patient asks "Will I die during a breathless attack?"

Feelings and Relationships with the Patient

B10   The patient seems to be denying the illness.

B11   Should you ever force a patient through denial?

B12   You are getting too involved with a patient.

B13   You find yourself distancing from a patient.

B14   The patient stops talking to you.

Communication with Relatives

B16   The relatives are angry.

B17   You wonder if the relatives are overstressed.

B18   The relatives are crying.

B19   You do not have enough time to talk with relatives.

B15   The patient wants to give up.

B20   Relatives ask you why the patient's treatment is not working.

B21   Relatives think the patient is in too much pain.

B22   Relatives ask you why the patient is not being fed.

B23   The relative asks you if he/she can sleep with the patient.

Communication around Death

B24   A staff member asks you: "Why don't we let this patient die in peace?"

B25   A patient dies - what do you say to relatives?

B26   A patient dies - what do you advise relatives to do?

B27   A patient has died - what do you say to other patients?

B28   A patient has a distressing death - what do you say to other patients?

Section C: Distressing Symptoms

Gastro-Intestinal problems

C1   The patient has halitosis.

C2   The patient is anorexic.

C3   The patient has a sore mouth.

C4   The patient complains of a dry mouth.

C5   The patient has dysphagia.

C6   The patient is nauseated.
C7   The patient is vomiting.
C8   The patient is constipated.
C9   The patient on opioids develops diarrhoea.
C10   Should you set up an IV infusion on a patient who is dying?

Other problems

C11   The patient has lymphoedema.
C12   The patient has a fungating breast lesion with foul odour: dressing changes cause pain and bleeding.
C13   The patient becomes immobile.
C14   The patient is confused.
C15   The patient is extremely restless.
C16   The patient is sweating excessively.
C17   The patient is twitching.
C18   The patient has itch.
C19   The patient is chronically fatigued.
C20   The patient is not sleeping.
C21   The patient has nightmares.
C22   The patient is dyspnoeic.
C23   You want to know the difference between clinical depression and acceptable sadness.

Section D: Context of Care

Patient Needs

D1   The patient wants to adopt 'complementary/alternative medicine' approaches.
D2   You do not feel equipped to help a patient with spiritual needs.
D3   The patient wants to make a will in hospital.
D4   The relatives cannot afford daily travel to visit the patient.

Ward Environment

D5   How can you make the hospital more like home?
D6   The relative wishes to help in the patient's care.
D7   What privacy is needed to discuss issues with a patient who has advanced cancer?
D8   You wonder if a dying patient should be moved to a side room?

Going home and Transfer

D9   The patient wants to go home for a few days.
D10   The relatives want to take the patient home.
D11   You need to arrange support for the patient and family at home.
D12   You are asked to arrange patient's transfer to a hospice.

Introduction

Introduction - About this Survival Package

Why the Need?

A person with advanced cancer, and their family, provide particular challenges to the hospital staff.

It is often in hospital settings that patients learn about their disease and begin the process of adjustment. In hospital

- the patient may want to talk to you about their prognosis.
- the patient and family may want to begin to plan for care at home.
- the family may want to share some really sad feelings with you.

Often, too, in hospital settings patients are faced with the physical effects of advanced cancer.

- In hospital settings patients can have particularly challenging and difficult pain problems that need to be solved, e.g. bone pain, nerve damage pain.
- Patients may return to hospital with the development of a new symptom, e.g. dyspnoea, intestinal obstruction.

In busy hospital settings, ward teams face the challenge of providing an appropriate environment for a patient to die with their family with them.

So How Will This Package Help You?

We know your time is pressurised and you need solutions to the new problems facing you in dealing with the advanced cancer patients and their families.

This programme is an easy to use resource. It is designed specifically to assist you with the decisions you will have to take, the questions you will face and the actions you will take. It is a survival package in palliative care.

It contains resource material which will help you to

- assess and manage the challenging problems of pain in advanced cancer.
- assess and manage the distressing symptoms of advanced disease.
- help you work with other professionals with different viewpoints.
- handle the more difficult questions you may be asked by patients or relatives.
- help patients adjust to changes in health.
- provide support for the patient facing imminent death.
- provide support for the patient's family.

How Can You Use This Package?

This reference book identifies 86 problems in palliative care.

It can be used in a number of ways. It will give you the information you need about the key problems in palliative care.

You may wish to use it

- when a new problem arises and you are uncertain about the most appropriate action, e.g. the patient develops a new pain.

- when you are asked to deal with a challenging communication issue for which you feel your training has not equipped you appropriately, e.g. breaking bad news to a patient.

- when you wish to review the quality of your management strategy for a patient, e.g. are the pain control drugs being used in the most effective way?

The book has a problem-based approach and a two-column layout as shown on Page 5. It comprises four sections - pain, communication, symptoms and context of care. Each section is divided again into subsections, dealing with specific problems.

A Main Heading Identifying the Problem Numbered Within Each Section

The Key Issues

A two column layout has been used throughout the book to facilitate learning at different levels.

The left hand column consists of four sub-headings, providing an action plan.

- ***What Do You Think About?***
- ***What Should You Try To Find Out?***
- ***What Do You Do?***
- ***How Do You Know If You Have Been Effective?***

Looking back and *forward* provide an opportunity to reflect on your practice and help you to look for similar problems emerging in other patients.

Items in bold are **cross-referenced.**

More Facts and Comments

This column provides you with more facts and further explanations. It may also outline some areas where views differ.

You will be given an opportunity to listen in to the experts. This is not ivory tower talk, but experienced practitioners sharing valuable insights into palliative care. A complete list of the literature referred to in the text is provided in the 'References' section page 347.

Quotes from patients, relatives and professionals in palliative care will also highlight certain issues.

Advance Organiser

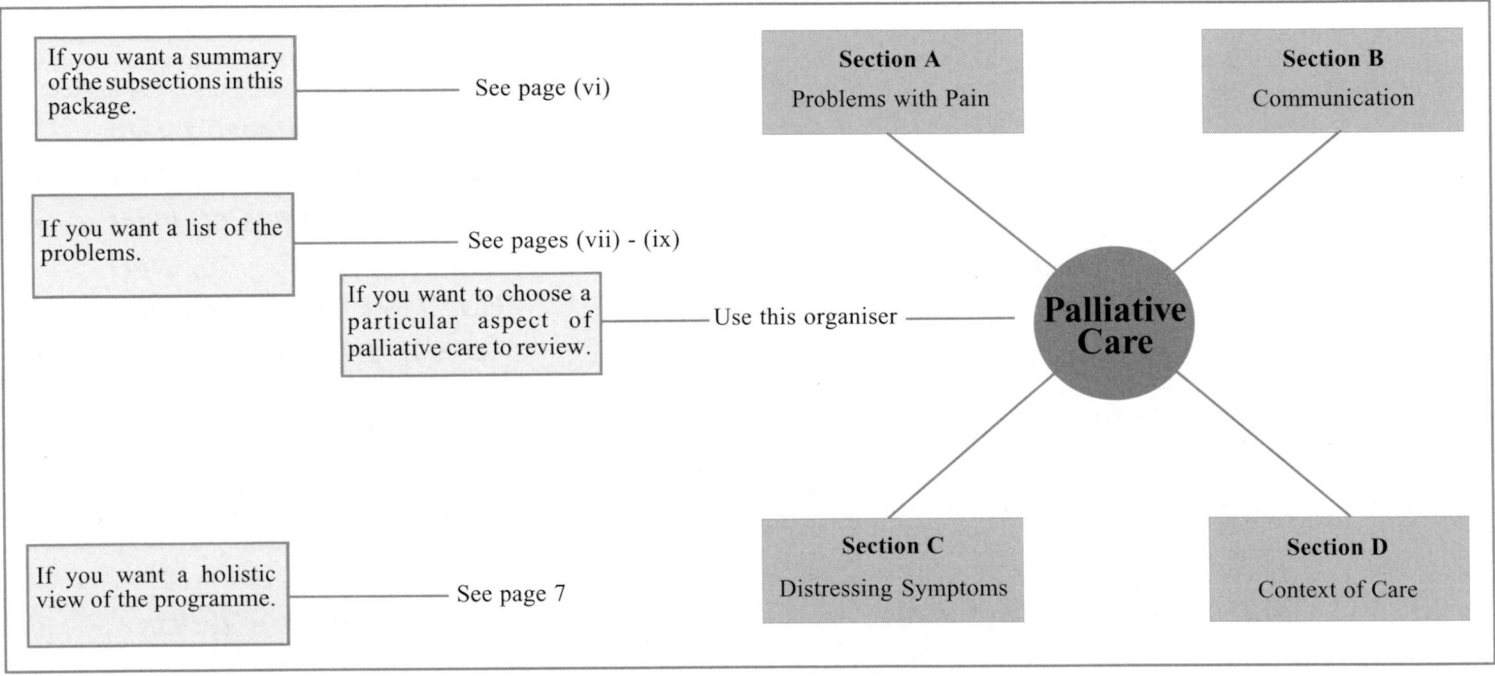

- If you want a summary of the subsections in this package. — See page (vi)
- If you want a list of the problems. — See pages (vii) - (ix)
- If you want to choose a particular aspect of palliative care to review. — Use this organiser — **Palliative Care**
- If you want a holistic view of the programme. — See page 7

Section A — Problems with Pain

Section B — Communication

Section C — Distressing Symptoms

Section D — Context of Care

Holistic View

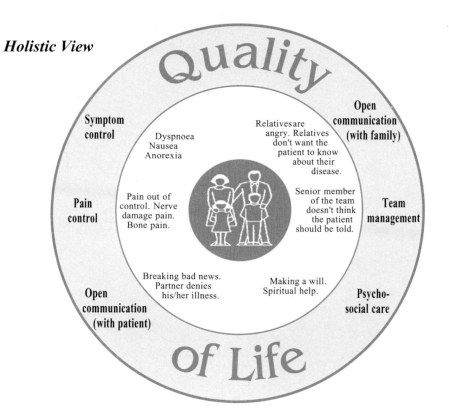

Quality

Symptom control

Open communication (with family)

Dyspnoea
Nausea
Anorexia

Relatives are angry. Relatives don't want the patient to know about their disease.

Pain control

Pain out of control. Nerve damage pain. Bone pain.

Senior member of the team doesn't think the patient should be told.

Team management

Breaking bad news. Partner denies his/her illness.

Making a will. Spiritual help.

Open communication (with patient)

Psycho-social care

of Life

In hospital or at home an improved quality of life can be achieved for the patient and the family. As the diagram shows, the patient and family are central. They are surrounded by problems, such as pain management, communication difficulties, distressing symptoms, psychological issues and team co-ordination. You can enable the patient and family to break through these barriers, to achieve quality of life - the outer circle.

Quality of life depends on effective pain management, open communication, adequate symptom control, psychosocial care and team planning.

Using a holistic approach, this MACPAC programme shows you how.

intentionally left blank

Section A - Pain

Section A: Pain - An Overview

Specific Patient Needs

- Wanting to be pain free but not 'flattened'
- Refusing analgesia

Specific Pain Experiences

- More than one pain
- Bone pain
- Nerve pain
- Difficult pains

Planning for Pain Relief

- Analgesics/co-analgesics
- Palliative radiotherapy
- Syringe drivers
- Pain relief clinics

Planning for Pain Relief

- You are being called repeatedly to reassess the patient's pain
- The ward team does not believe in high dose opioids
- Your colleagues think you are overstating the patient's experience of pain

A1   *Assessing a Patient's Pain*

The Key Issues

What Do You Think About?

Published reports indicate that about 70% of cancer patients are experiencing pain or being treated for it. Pain in cancer could be due to many causes other than malignancy. The cancer patient may also experience different kinds of pain. Therefore, in assessing pain in advanced cancer you have to consider

- the cause of the pain, and
- the possibility that the patient might have more than one pain.

What Should You Try To Find Out?

- The site, nature, distribution and duration of the pain(s).
- What does the patient assume is the cause of the pain?
- Make an appropriate examination of the patient.

More Facts and Comments

Pain in cancer can be
- caused by the primary cancer or secondary spread (by far the most common type of pain);
- related to the cancer or debility (e.g. muscle spasm, **constipation** or bed sores);
- related to treatment (e.g. chronic post-operative scar pain, **stomatitis** or resulting from chemotherapy);
- caused by a concurrent disorder (e.g. spondylosis, arthritis).

Many patients with advanced cancer have multiple pains that may relate to several of these categories.

Pain in cancer has a variety of causes. Cancer itself is the sole cause of pain in only about half of the patients.
R G Twycross (1990)

It is essential to get the patient involved in the assessment and management of their pain. Accurate recording of the patient's pain is important. Staff and some patients find assessment charts useful for recording site and severity of pains.

Doctors caring for cancer patients need, as far as possible, to acquire the skill of determining the cause of the pain on the basis of diagnostic probabilities. Invasive investigations are increasingly contraindicated as patients move closer to death.
R G Twycross (1989)

The Key Issues	*More Facts and Comments*

- What treatment has the patient had for pain, including: drugs, dosage, frequency of administration and non-drug measures?
- Order appropriate investigations.

What Do You Do?

- Make a diagnosis of the cause of each pain.
- Establish some *realistic goal* with the patient, e.g.
  - increase the hours of pain-free sleep,
  - relieve the pain when at rest,
  - relieve pain on standing and during activity.
- Treat each pain specifically.
- Review the patient regularly.

The goal of palliative cancer care may be summed up by the word rehabilitation: helping patients to achieve and to maintain their maximum physical, emotional, spiritual, vocational and social potential, however limited this may be as a result of disease progression.

The Key Issues	*More Facts and Comments*

How Do You Know If You Have Been Effective?

Effectiveness can be determined if you have managed to establish

- a degree of pain control,
- the presence or absence of side-effects of treatment.

Looking back

It is important to determine as accurately as possible the cause of the pain. This often has major implications for treatment.

Looking forward

An awareness of common causes of pain, such as muscle pain, is necessary to prevent many erroneous conclusions which lead to prescribing the wrong analgesic. Similarly helpful is some knowledge of the patterns of metastatic spread.

When pain is wrongly assumed to be due to the cancer, it tends to be invested with all the negative implications of cancer pain, such as the imagined difficulty in controlling it or the feeling that this is the end. All that is required is an informed knowledge when we are assessing the patient's pain.

A2   *The Patient's Subjective Experience of Pain*

The Key Issues	*More Facts and Comments*

What Do You Think About?

Pain is always subjective. Each individual interprets the severity of pain through experiences related to injury in early life. Pain is always unpleasant and therefore an emotional experience. In assessing the patient's subjective experience of pain you have to think about

- low pain threshold
- psychological factors in pain
- the concept of 'total pain'.

The easy assumption that the severity of pain is proportional to the extent of injury runs counter to both personal experience and clinical practice. A small boy may sustain a fracture while playing football and barely mention it. Similar degrees of arthritis appear to cripple one patient but, in another, be compatible with active life. Such common situations emphasise the fact that pain is subjective and is related both to tissue damage and to emotional factors. Pain is a somatopsychic experience.
M Baines (1990)

The concept of 'total pain', first coined by Saunders in 1967, encompasses all the elements that contribute to the patient's suffering. It consists of four integrated components:

- physical
- psychological
- social
- spiritual.

The identification and proper management of each of these components will help:

- better control of the physical symptoms
- achievement of the main objective of palliative care: *the well-being of the whole person.*

The Key Issues	More Facts and Comments

More Facts and Comments

More about total pain

Saunders C (ed). Hospice and palliative care - An interdisciplinary approach. London, Edward Arnold, 1990.

For true multidisciplinary palliative care to be effective, there needs to be an overlap between the roles of team members. It is important to acknowledge that the patient and their family are part of the team. In the sphere of palliation there are few clear cut best choices of care, the implication being that, where possible, the individual's own wishes are important treatment indicators. However, to include the patient in decision making requires clear and open **communication** among all members of the health care team.

Pain is what the patient says it is and exists when he says it does.
M McCaffery (1983)

The Key Issues

What Should You Try To Find Out?

- Patient's past experience of pain.
- Patient's understanding of their pain.
- Other factors influencing patient's perception of pain, e.g. **fear of addiction**, anger, anxiety.

What Do You Do?

- Review the cause of patient's pain.
- Involve the patient in the management of his/her pain.

The Key Issues	*More Facts and Comments*

How Do You Know If You Have Been Effective?

Consider additional information about patient's pain behaviour from family and other hospital staff

- exaggerating, or
- tolerant?

Looking back

Ask yourself

- "How many times have I considered pain as a separate physical entity detached from the patient's personal feelings, fear and anxiety?"

- "How many times have I been successful in controlling pain in such situations?"

Few patients talk with their doctors, rather doctors and patients talk at each other. Of all health professionals, the nurse is unique in having close, trusted, prolonged contact. This position is one of enormous responsibility and opportunity.
P D Wall (1987)

The Key Issues

Looking forward
What are you going to do in the future with other patients in your care?

It is important to realise that a sense of hopelessness and the fear of impending death add to the total suffering of the cancer patient.

More Facts and Comments

A3   *The Patient Has More Than One Pain*

What Do You think About?

Pain in advanced cancer is caused by a number of factors. These include tissue destruction, pressure, trauma, neurological involvement, muscle spasm, infection, ischaemia or disturbed metabolic function. Each pain may have special characteristics which herald it at a different stage of evolution of the pathological process. Each may also require different methods of control. Having diagnosed the causes of pain, it is pertinent then to consider these questions.

- Is the treatment offered appropriate for all pains?
- Which pain needs specific treatment, e.g. co-analgesics (adjuvant drugs) or non-drug measures?
- What changes need to be made in the treatment?

In advanced cancer, most patients with pain have multiple pains. A prospective survey of 100 cancer patients with pain was carried out by Twycross and Fairfield (1982). A total of 303 anatomically distinct pains was garnered, an average of three per patient. Eighty had more than one pain; 34 had four or more.

Opioids are of limited value for certain pains and sometimes they are contraindicated.
R G Twycross (1989)

Co-analgesics (adjuvants)
These are a series of compounds of different chemical structure. Some have no conventional analgesic activity. Nevertheless, their actions may complement or supplant conventional analgesics. For example
- coricosteroids, e.g. dexamethasone, in nerve compression, spinal cord compression, headaches due to raised intracranial pressure, and occasionally in painful lymphoedema and painful hepatomegaly
- non-steroidal anti-inflammatory drugs (NSAIDs) in bone pain
- anticonvulsants in lancinating (shooting, stabbing) nerve pain

The Key Issues	*More Facts and Comments*
	• antidepressants in dysaesthetic pain (eg superficial burning) nerve pain • muscle relaxants in pain of skeletal muscle spasm • antibiotics in pain due to infection. **Two rules for use of co-analgesics** The use of these drugs depends on careful assessment of the patient's symptoms and the clinical signs. They should not be prescribed routinely. The choice of a drug is always dictated by the need of the individual patient. *Co-analgesia is an important part of any therapeutic approach and the co-analgesics (adjuvants) are a varied and interesting group of compounds. Almost all have no conventional analgesic activity but nevertheless their actions may complement or supplant accepted analgesics.* *Ray Corcoran, (1991).*
• Does palliative radiotherapy have a role to play?	**Palliative radiotherapy** Short courses of radiotherapy may have an important role in treating pain of primary and secondary cancer. Such courses should not produce side effects. The advice of a radiotherapist and oncologist or clinical oncologist should be sought.

The Key Issues	*More Facts and Comments*

Pain due to bony secondaries responds in up to 90% of cases, with complete control of pain in 50-60% of cases.

In addition the following pains may respond to palliative radiotherapy:
- pain due to local recurrence, e.g. in rectal cancer or other pelvic tumours,
- pain due to Pancoast's tumour of the lung.

Palliative radiotherapy may have other useful effects in treating patients with advanced cancer:
- stopping haematuria, in advanced bladder cancer,
- halting haemoptysis in lung cancer,
- allowing healing of a fungating breast cancer.

What Should You Try To Find Out?

Review
- each pain and its likely cause
- the **response of pain** to treatment received.

The Key Issues	*More Facts and Comments*

What Do You Do?

Consider

- what other investigations are needed, e.g. X-ray or bone scan
- the use of co-analgesics (adjuvant drugs)
- adequate explanation for the patient and family.

Explaining the cause of each pain is of fundamental importance.
R G Twycross (1990)

How Do You Know If You Have Been Effective?

- Have you established the cause of different pains and prescribed accordingly?
- Has there been a significant response to the new treatment?
- Have the patient and family understood what is going on?

A4 *The Patient Refuses Analgesia When in Severe Pain*

Key Issues	*More Facts and Comments*

What Do You Think About?

In this critical situation you have to think about the reasons behind the patient's refusal.

- Is it fear of cancer?
- Is it fear of drugs, e.g. fear of addiction?
- Is it the patient's mental state, e.g. **confusion**?
- Is it other influences on the patient, e.g. family, other patients, other staff?

We also have to think of ways to improve the patient's compliance.

What Should You Try To Find Out?

- Patient's understanding of their pain.
- What fears do they have about their disease?
- What fears do they have about analgesics in particular?
- What other opinions about analgesics have they had?

The right to treatment, or to refuse it, raises difficult questions. Interpreted too narrowly, it seems to oblige the health care team to maintain life for as long as possible without regard to its quality. The professionals have the responsibility to interpret treatment, including the use of analgesics, in terms of what is in the best interests of the patient. This entails establishing a dialogue with the patient to explore their fears, expectations and the influences of others on their decision. A strategy should be adopted to explain what is best for them from a professional point of view and in such a way as to reflect empathy and sympathy. Professionals may have to persist with treatment in certain circumstances if the patient is not thought competent to decide.

Key Issues	More Facts and Comments

What Do You Do?

Explanation is an essential part of treatment.

- Explain the nature of pain to the patient.
- Describe the experience of other patients with the treatment that is offered.
- Explain the likely side-effects.
- Discuss treatment plans with others involved, e.g. family and other staff.

How Do You Know If You Have Been Effective?

A positive change in the patient's attitude to treatment is not only an indication of your effectiveness. It also shows the importance of teamwork and active involvement of the patient and family in decision making and treatment plans.

An ethical dilemma arises when patients refuse medication. Here we sum up expert views on the subject.

- It is unwise to conceal the medication, eg in food or drink, because this may heighten the patient's mistrust if discovered.
- Firm coaxing by a trusted member of family or staff may suffice.
- Effective communication between staff, patient and family can allay much of the possible fear and anger.

As far as opioids are concerned, psychological dependence (addiction) does not occur when these drugs are being used to treat pain. Fear of addiction is based on a misunderstanding of the term and is an empty fear.
G W Hanks (1988)

A5   *You are Being Called Repeatedly to Reassess the Patient's Pain*

Sometimes you are called repeatedly to review a particular patient. Surely there is a reason for that, and you have to find it.

What Do You Think About?

Is it due to
- inadequate initial assessment?
- incorrect diagnosis?
- inappropriate or inadequate treatment?
- other unrecognised factors, e.g. fear, anger, unfulfilled psychosocial needs on the part of the patient, family or carers?
- poor patient compliance caused by fears of side-effects.

Remember:
- Most cancer patients have a **number of pains.**
- Every pain is not cancer pain.
- Not all pains respond to strong opioids.
- Some pains require adjuvant (**co-analgesic**) drugs or non-drug therapy (e.g. radiotherapy in bone pain due to bone metastases).
- Continuous pain requires continuous analgesia.
- If an analgesic ceases to be effective prescribe a stronger analgesic.
- Fear of addiction to strong opioids in patients with cancer pain is unfounded.
- Pain is not just somatic. It is a complex psychosomatic experience: perception of pain can be exaggerated by worries, fear and anger.

Delineating the PQRST characteristics of pain (Palliative and Provocative factors, Quality, Radiation, Severity and Temporal factors) is only the first step in assessment. Diagnosis needs an understanding of pathology, neuroanatomy, referred pain, patterns of metastatic spread, knowledge of common muscle pain syndromes, together with an informed imagination. Also important is the concept of total pain.
R G Twycross (1990)

| *Key Issues* | *More Facts and Comments* |

What Should You Try To Find Out?

What treatment was previously prescribed?

Was this treatment appropriate?

Has it been taken by the patient?

Is something (e.g. **vomiting**) preventing drug absorption?

What is the **patient's experience of pain** and its effect on movement and sleep?

What are other peoples' assessments of the situation?

What Do You Do?

Involve the patient in assessment.   Pain charts may be helpful.

- Ask the patient to mark all his or her pains on the body diagram on the chart or on a hand drawn sketch if the pain charts are not available.
- Label each site of pain with a letter (A, B, C etc).

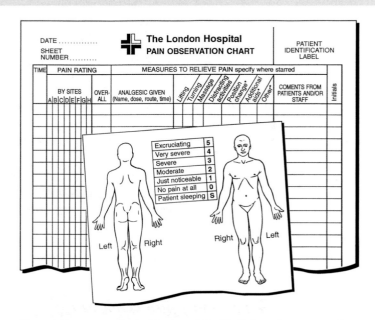

Excerpts from a pain chart. Courtesy of Jennifer Raiman, Department of Clinical Pharmacology and Therapeutics, Royal London Hospital Medical College, Cancer Relief Macmillan Fund.

Key Issues	*More Facts and Comments*

Key Issues

- Rate the severity of each pain e.g. excruciating (5), very severe (4), severe (3), moderate (2), or just noticeable (1).
- Note the time and dose of any given analgesic and nursing care or action taken to ease pain.
- Note the response of each pain to the above measures since last observation.

Review diagnosis.

Review the treatment provided.

Plan treatment with the patient, **setting realistic and achievable goals of pain control.**

Get help from colleagues if you cannot improve pain control.

Explain the situation to the patient, family and nursing staff.

More Facts and Comments

"*Pain observation and assessment charts provide an opportunity for improving communication about pain by using a patient-centred method of regular assessment and review.*

They focus attention on the mechanisms of different pains and provide evidence on what relieves them, by recording each site of pain separately.

They made readily available in one place information that is useful when taking decisions about the management of pain.

You are likely to find them most helpful when you know that a patient's pain is a problem or you think it may be."

Jennifer Raiman, Medical Programme Advisor, Cancer Relief Macmillan Fund

Key Issues	**More Facts and Comments**

How Do You Know If You Have Been Effective?

A logical approach to assessment and reassessment of the patient's pain is the key to a successful control of symptoms.

Looking back

Have you provided enough time to listen to the patient?

Have you considered all the factors that could provoke and exaggerate pain?

Looking forward

Palliative care is a team approach and so much depends on effective teamwork. Nurses and family can tell you about the patient's needs, fears and worries. When the patient feels that you are giving more time, he or she will entrust you with feelings. Help from other team members, the chaplain or a social worker, may provide a breakthrough in difficult situations.

The simplest and most reliable index of pain is the patient's verbal report.
I C Lasagna (1960)

Key Issues	More Facts and Comments

What Do You Think About?

It is quite understandable how bad one feels when a patient's pain is out of control.

In this situation one has to think rationally.

- Is it me?
- Have I assessed the pain adequately?
- Have I prescribed the appropriate and adequate treatment?
- Have I considered the concept of **total pain**?
- Have I sought the necessary help?
- Is it the disease?
- Has a **new pain** developed that does not respond to current treatment?
- Is it the patient?
- Is it due to poor compliance?

One-third of advanced cancer patients do not experience pain. For the remaining two-thirds, pain relief can be achieved in about nine out of ten patients.

"*The pain is driving me crazy. I can't think about anything else.*"
A patient

"*It is all pain!*"
A patient

In a study by F Takeda (1986), 'complete' pain relief was reported by 87% of the patients, while 'acceptable' relief was achieved in a further 9% and 'partial' relief in the remaining 4%. It must be emphasised that a high degree of pain control can be achieved by non-specialists, simply through applying basic principles.

Key Issues	*More Facts and Comments*

What Should You Try To Find Out?

- What previous **assessment** was made?
- What treatment has been offered?
- Has the treatment been given to the patient?
- Are there new factors contributing to the severity of pain? Examples include
  - new pains
  - progression of disease
  - other causes, e.g. **vomiting** interfering with drug absorption.

What Do You Do?

- Reassess the patient.
- Establish short-term goals in pain control, e.g. a pain-free night's sleep.

Accurate assessment and reassessment of cancer pain are central to effective symptom control.
Ray Corcorcan, (1991).

Key Issues	*More Facts and Comments*

Key Issues

- Prescribe appropriate treatment and ensure its administration.

More Facts and Comments

Remember:
- continuous pain requires continuous therapy.
- some pains respond only partially, or not at all, to opioids.
- **co-analgesics** such as antidepressants, anticonvulsants, NSAIDs and steroids are more effective in controlling some pains (see **nerve damage** and **bone pains).**
- non-drug therapy, e.g. palliative radiotherapy can help in certain pains. The advice of a radiotherapist and oncologist is essential. (See **bone pain.**)

There are four basic principles to adopt in opioid-responsive pains.

1   By mouth whenever feasible
Oral morphine is the strong opioid of choice for cancer pain. It has a plasma half-life of 2 - 2.5 hours. Apart from patients with renal failure, there is no danger of drug accumulation. In practice, the choice of prescribing lies between aqueous solution of morphine sulphate/hydrochloride (four-hourly), immediate release tablets (four-hourly) and slow release tablets (twelve-hourly).

2   By the clock
Analgesics should be given on a regular basis. The next dose is given before the effect of the previous one has fully worn off.

Key Issues	*More Facts and Comments*

3   By the ladder

The WHO has established an analgesic ladder, based on the premise: "If a drug ceases to be effective, do not switch to an alternative drug of similar strength, but prescribe a drug that is definitely stronger".

The analgesic ladder for cancer pain management

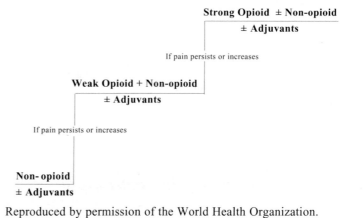

Reproduced by permission of the World Health Organization.

Key Issues	More Facts and Comments

More Facts and Comments

4   For the individual

The dose of morphine required by any one cancer patient is very variable and must be individualised. *There is no ceiling dose.* The dose ultimately required must be attained by titration of the dose against the intensity of the individual's pain. Start by a small four-hourly dose of aqueous morphine and work up from there. A commonly used sequence is that suggested by Twycross and Lack (1984), ie 5-10-15-20-30-40-60-80-100-120-200-240 mg four-hourly etc.

In general about two-thirds of patients will not need more than the equivalent of 30 mg of morphine four-hourly (180 mg/day). However, that leaves a third of patients who are going to need doses in excess of that. Patients who will need very high doses, more than a gram a day, are relatively rare. It is not right to have any sort of arbitrary limit in mind. As long as you go on getting an increase in response, you can go on increasing the dose.
G W Hanks (1988)

Key Issues

Review after a short period, e.g. one hour.

- Consult, when necessary, with, e.g.
  - the pain specialist at your hospital
  - the palliative care specialist at the hospice nearest you
  - other specialists - surgeons, radiotherapist, and clinical oncologist, physiotherapist, etc.
- Confidently and realistically explain your treatment plan to the patient and family. Allay their apprehension and fears.

| **Key Issues** | **More Facts and Comments** |

How Do You Know If You Have Been Effective?

Nothing would vouch for your success more than seeing a patient having a reprieve from pain.

Looking back

Perhaps the uncontrolled pain was due to fear of increasing the opioid dose or **fear of addiction.** Both are unfounded. The rule is to tailor the dose to the individual.

Looking forward

If you adopt the basic principles of pain control, you will achieve relief in eight or nine out of every ten patients.

"*Last night's sleep was a gift.***"**
A patient

Fear of addiction - A4   **Assessing Pain**

Key Issues	*More Facts and Comments*

What Do You Think About?

The possibilities to consider are that the new pain may be due to

- progression of cancer
- malignant debility
- treatment (side-effect)
- a concurrent non-malignant cause.

The response of that new pain to opioids may be

- only partial
- no response.

Do all cancer pains respond equally to opioids?
The answer is 'No'. From a pharmacological point of view, pain in cancer falls into three categories.

1   Opioid responsive pains
- visceral pain - prescribe opioid.

2   Opioid semi-responsive pains, e.g.
- **bone pain** - prescribe non-steroidal anti-inflammatory drug (NSAID) + opioid + palliative radiotherapy.
- nerve compression - prescribe corticosteroid + opioid.

3   Opioid resistant pains, e.g.
- **nerve damage pain** - prescribe anticonvulsant and/or antidepressant.
- muscle spasm - prescribe muscle relaxant.

The importance of classifying cancer pains into opioid responsive, semi-responsive and resistant lies in the fact that it reminds doctors that opioids are of limited value for certain pains, and that sometimes they are contra-indicated.
R G Twycross (1989)

Morphine alone is not the panacea for all cancer pains. Adjuvant therapy is often necessary, depending on the nature of the pain.
M K Kearney (1990)

Key Issues	*More Facts and Comments*

What Should You Try To Find Out?

History taking, physical examination and appropriate investigations clarify

- site, nature, distribution and duration of the new pain
- aggravating and relieving factors
- motor weakness and sensory deficits
- visceral dysfunction
- state of pressure points, particularly in debilitated patients
- metastases, particularly bony
- state of anxiety and **depression**.

Key Issues	*More Facts and Comments*

What Do You Do?

Prescribe the appropriate co-analgesic.

Consult with radiotherapist, **pain relief clinic**, physiotherapist, etc. about

- **palliative radiotherapy**
- nerve blocks, e.g. coeliac plexus block in painful pancreatic, gastric or biliary cancers
- relaxation/massage in muscle spasm.

Explain the situation and proposed treatment to patient.

Reassess the response of the new pain to treatment.

Pain relief clinics

These are now available in most districts and are principally run by the Anaesthetic Service. Pain relief clinics have a remit in pain control in non-cancer and cancer patients. For cancer patients, pain relief clinics are useful in diagnosis and management of neurogenic pain and pain uncontrolled by radiotherapy or opioids.

Key Issues	*More Facts and Comments*

How Do You Know If You Have Been Effective?

This will be evident when you have achieved

- an acceptable level of pain control, and
- boosting of the patient's morale and coping ability.

Looking forward

The value of a differential diagnosis in the effective treatment of cancer pain cannot be overestimated. Diagnosis needs an understanding of pathology, neuroanatomy and referred pain, and patterns of metastatic spread. Needless to say, recognition of the concept of **total pain** is also important in planning treatment and allaying the patient's suffering.

A8 *The Patient Has Bone Pain*

Key Issues	*More Facts and Comments*

What Do You Think About?

This may be a new phase of the illness, due to bony metastases - a common cause of cancer pain.

You have to consider also the possibility of a pathological fracture. This could be the first indication of bone metastases.

Of the tumours that produce osteolytic lesions and weakness or fracture of the bones, breast tumours are by far the most common, accounting for nearly half the fractures seen. Bronchial carcinoma, prostatic carcinoma and myelomatosis are also common, but almost any primary tumour can occasionally produce a pathological fracture.

What Should You Try To Find Out?

Is there any local tenderness over the affected bone?

Is there any involvement of the spine, evidenced by back pain or signs of cord compression, e.g. urinary disturbance, weakness of the leg?

Metastatic disease of the spine produces two major problems. First, pain may be severe, due to expansion of tumour within the vertebrae which may also produce fractures and collapse. Second, erosion of a vertebral body can cause mechanical instability of the spine at one or more levels. Neurological deficit due to compression of the spinal cord, cauda equina or nerve roots could result from either expanding extradural deposits or spinal instability.

Key Issues	*More Facts and Comments*

Confirm the diagnosis by

- plain radiographs of the whole bone involved, and
- a radioisotope scan of the whole skeleton. The scan will also define any further occult lesions.

What Do You Do?

Key elements in bone pain management are:

- radiotherapy - treatment of choice,
- symptomatic drug treatment, and, sometimes,
- orthopaedic intervention.

However, management of bone pain should follow this schedule.

1   Immediate control of pain

Use a non-steroidal anti-inflammatory drug (NSAID), e.g. aspirin 300-900 mg 4-6 hourly (maximum daily dose 4g) naproxen 500 mg twice daily or ketoprofen slow release 200 mg daily.

It is important to realise that bone pain is **semi-responsive to morphine.** In metastatic bone disease a high local concentration of prostaglandins is often produced by the tumour cells. **NSAID**s provide pain relief by blocking prostaglandin biosynthesis. They also have anti-inflammatory and antipyretic effects.

Key Issues	*More Facts and Comments*

Morphine should be titrated to pain

Where there is impending *spinal cord compression*, prescribe dexamethasone, 16 mg daily in divided doses, pending consultation with a radiotherapist, orthopaedic surgeon or neurosurgeon. This consultation is *a matter of urgency* and should be sought immediately. Paraplegia even in a patient with weeks to live is a disaster.

Also contact the orthopaedic surgeon without delay if there is a pathological fracture of a long bone or vertebral involvement.

Steroids, especially dexamethasone, have proved very useful in the acute management of incipient spinal cord compression, as they may buy time whilst a full assessment is made.
J S Albert, (1989).

Role of orthopaedic surgeon

- Fixation of pathological fracture
  - external
  - internal.
- Decompression of the spinal cord.
- Stabilisation of the vertebral column.

Key Issues

2   Long-term control of pain

Palliative radiotherapy is the treatment of choice. Important points are

- has the patient's tumour responded to radiotherapy before?
- has the area been irradiated before?
- obtain the opinion of the radiotherapist and clinical oncologist without delay.

Hormonal treatment may be required e.g. for prostatic and breast carcinomas. Advice from the oncologist should be sought.

More Facts and Comments

Role of palliative radiotherapy
As well as giving rapid pain control, the structural integrity of the bone may improve in the medium term with recalcification at the site of the metastases.

External beam radiotherapy is the best treatment for *localised* metastatic bone pain. A single dose seems to be as effective as fractionated treatment and is clearly more convenient.

Palliative hemibody irradiation is an effective and simple palliative treatment for *widespread* symptomatic bony metastases. It is most effective in those tumours with a relatively *long natural history,* such as carcinoma of the prostate and some breast carcinomas. The technique is simple, provides an economical use of resources and saves the patient repeated visits to hospital.

" *The local pain due to bone metastases from any primary site is relieved in up to 90% of cases by a short palliative course of radiotherapy: in many cases by a single fraction given on one attendance. Widespread metastases, on the other hand, may respond to hemibody radiotherapy. The upper or the lower hemibody can be treated with a single fraction of radiotherapy.* **"**

R H MacDougall, Consultant Radiation Oncologist

Key Issues	*More Facts and Comments*

3   **At all times**, the patient
- should be reassured that treatment is directed to relief of pain, restoration of mobility and return to independence with the minimum of delay.
- should also understand that surgery for metastatic bone disease is not expected to prolong life or be in any way curative.

How Do You Know If You Have Been Effective?

Reassess pain approximately one week after irradiation. Relief may not be experienced for two weeks.

Looking back

Have you prescribed NSAIDs soon enough and in proper doses to achieve pain control, pending the effect of palliative radiotherapy?

Key Issues	More Facts and Comments

What Do You Think About?

Malignant infiltration leading to

- nerve damage
- spinal cord damage
- compression of cord or nerve(s) by the tumour.

Treatment-related nerve damage caused by

- radiotherapy
- chemotherapy.

Nerve damage pain characteristics

Pain caused by damage to a nerve or to the spinal cord may take several patterns. It may present as *hyperaesthesia* or different types of *dysaesthesiae*, ranging from the superficial burning to stabbing, shooting or lancinating pains. It may also present as a deep aching pain, if there is an element of compression. Pain with a dermatomal distribution indicates nerve root involvement. Light touch exacerbates pain, and the patient may be unable to bear clothing against affected area. There may be associated neurological signs, with or without areas of numbness (hypoaesthesia), in the region of the pain.

Response to conventional analgesics, including opioids is usually poor. However, the use of a tricyclic antidepressant drug and/or an anticonvulsant drug may help.

Deafferentation pain is a particularly confusing term which means different things to different people. It is an umbrella term encompassing a variety of quite different clinical syndromes.

Nerve damage pain is a preferable term and much more easily understood in this context.
G W Hanks (1988)

Key Issues	*More Facts and Comments*

What Should You Try To Find Out?

- Pain characteristics.
- Ability to sleep at night.
- Neurological deficits.

What Do You Do?

Explain to the patient

- nature of nerve damage pain,
- how it responds poorly to conventional pain-killers,
- need to phase out unhelpful medication, and
- need to start him or her on antidepressant and/or anticonvulsant as a co-analgesic.

Assure the patient with pain-related insomnia that, given time, the new treatment should help them achieve a good night's sleep.

Key Issues	*More Facts and Comments*

Key Issues

Prescribe the appropriate drug.
- Burning pain.

  The antidepressant amitriptyline - starting dose 10-25 mg in a single dose at bedtime and increase slowly, as required, to 50-75 mg.

- Stabbing and shooting pain.

  The anticonvulsant carbamazepine - an initial dose of 100 mg a day increasing by 100 mg every 3-4 days to a maximum of 400 mg twice daily.

More Facts and Comments

Side-effects of amitriptyline include
- dry mouth
- constipation
- urinary retention
- light-headedness
- confusion.

Care is required in patients with glaucoma.

Side-effects of carbamazepine include
- nausea
- vomiting
- ataxia
- dizziness
- lethargy
- confusion.

Key Issues	*More Facts and Comments*

Key Issues

- Multiple pains.

You may require to prescribe both amitriptyline and carbamazepine.

Assess the pain regularly.

Look out for side-effects.

If you fail to control nerve damage pain, consult the **pain relief clinic** or **hospice.**

How Do You Know If You Have Been Effective?

Has the patient achieved

- a good night's sleep?
- a satisfactory level of symptom control?

More Facts and Comments

The patient must be monitored as often as possible to ensure that treatment continues to match the pain and to minimise side-effects.

Key Issues	More Facts and Comments

Looking back

Reflect on how this unrelenting pain, with associated sleeplessness, can exaggerate the patient's anxiety and demoralise him or her.

Looking forward

Remember that the patient at this stage will need more support.

An early control of this distressing symptom will not only boost the patient's morale, but will also enhance his or her confidence in your ability.

A10 *The Patient on High Doses of Opioids is Still in Pain*

Key Issues	More Facts and Comments

What Do You Think About?

Is the patient getting the opioid as prescribed?

Patients for whom high doses of opioids have been prescribed are frequently fearful of taking these drugs. They often expect side-effects such as nausea/vomiting or constipation. They may also fear addiction.

It is important to explain to the patient any anticipated side-effects and how they will be managed. The patient should understand that nausea and vomiting caused by opioids usually disappear within seven to ten days and that the appropriate laxative will be prescribed for constipation. They should also understand that fear of addiction to opioids in cancer pain relief is unfounded.

Psychological dependence (addiction) does not occur in patients who are prescribed morphine for cancer pain, provided it is used in the context of total patient care.

Physical dependence develops in most patients who have taken an opioid regularly for more than three to four weeks. This is not a problem for dying patients, as they will continue on regular morphine until they die.
R G Twycross and S A Lack (1989)

Is the opioid being absorbed?

Sustained release preparations of morphine may fail to control pain in some patients because of poor absorption.

Key Issues	*More Facts and Comments*

Does the patient need an extra dose of opioid for the **breakthrough pain**?

Remember the following points when prescribing an opioid for a breakthrough pain:

- the dose of opioid for a breakthrough pain is equivalent to *one-sixth* of the total 24-hour dose. In other words, if a patient is on 100 mg, twice daily, of morphine sulphate sustained release tablets, the dose for the breakthrough pain should be 30 mg of morphine sulphate solution or tablets.

- if the breakthrough dose is used frequently, reassess the patient to find out the reason. This is usually due to progression of the disease.

- the breakthrough dose should be taken into account when the prescription of the main analgesic is reviewed.

- remember to increase the breakthrough dose when you increase the dose of the main analgesic.

- if the patient is on **continuous subcutaneous infusion**, the breakthrough dose of opioid should be given subcutaneously.

Key Issues	*More Facts and Comments*
Is the opioid appropriate for the type of pain that the patient is experiencing?	Bone pain, smooth muscle pain, pain from raised intracranial pressure and nerve damage pain are better managed with the use of **co-analgesics** than with opioids alone.

Remember the concept of **total pain**. Are there other factors contributing to the patient's complaint of pain?

What Should You Try To Find Out?

Establish the answers to the above questions by taking a careful history from the patient and the patient's carers.

What Do You Do?

Review the assumptions made about the **cause of the patient's pain**.

Examine the patient again.

Review the results of previous investigations that may help in the management of pain, e.g. X-rays, bone scans.

Request any further investigations that would be helpful, e.g. X-rays, bone scans.

Key Issues	More Facts and Comments

Consider the use of co-analgesic drugs, such as dexamethasone, in headaches due to increased intracranial pressure.

Consider the use of any non-drug measures, such as radiotherapy in bone metastases.

How Do You Know If You Have Been Effective?
Review the patient after a short interval and again after 24 hours.

Liaise with other professionals, e.g. radiotherapist, physiotherapist, pain relief clinic staff.

Looking back
Have you identified the cues to the patient's pain from the patient, the patient's family and your colleagues' statements?

Looking forward
How can you plan for future analgesic needs?

A11   *The Patient is 'Flattened' with Morphine*

The Key Issues

What Do You Think About?

There are several possibilities that could induce this condition.

- Is the patient also on a sedative?
- Does the patient have a morphine responsive pain?
- Is the dose of morphine too high?
- Has the dose of morphine been escalated too rapidly?
- Has the patient's condition deteriorated and with it their ability to metabolise morphine?
- Has the pain been relieved by another means, e.g. radiotherapy or nerve block?

What Should You Try To Find Out?

Establish the dose of drug being prescribed and the duration of treatment.

Check that this is the dose the patient has received.

Review any other concomitant therapy.

More Facts and Comments

Sedation is a very common side-effect of opioid drugs. Most patients develop selective tolerance to the effects of opioid drugs, with the exception of analgesia and constipation. If a patient had been maintained on a dose of an opioid, one would expect the sedative effect to diminish after 48-72 hours. If the dose of an opioid is escalated rapidly, sedation will be a bigger problem. The sedative effect of drugs used in combination may be additive, e.g. **benzodiazepines, cyclizine.**

The Key Issues	**More Facts and Comments**

Review any recent biochemical tests, particularly of renal function.

What Do You Do?

Reduce or stop any other **sedative drugs** that are being prescribed.

If the patient's pain is controlled, omit the next dose of morphine and reduce subsequent doses appropriately.

Explain your management to the family and nursing colleagues.

How Do You Know If You Have Been Effective?

Review the patient after three to four hours and again after 24 hours. Look for signs of recovery from the sedation.

The clearance of morphine is not affected by impaired renal function, but accumulation of morphine glucuronides occurs. It is likely that accumulation of M-6-G (Morphine-6-glucuronide) is responsible for the increased effects of toxicity of morphine in patients with renal failure.
G W Hanks (1989)

"*It is rarely necessary to use drugs which antagonise the effects of morphine such as naloxone. Patients who are oversedated with morphine will normally recover if the dose is reduced or, if necessary, stopped.*"
W M O'Neill, Consultant in Palliative Medicine

The Key Issues	*More Facts and Comments*

Looking back

It is essential, in prescribing for a patient with advanced cancer, to give the opioid in a sufficient dose to control pain.

It is also important to check the side-effects of other prescribed drugs to avoid any unnecessary potentiation of sedative effects.

Looking forward

Assessment of the progress of cancer, particularly liver metastases and renal impairment, should be undertaken regularly.

The Key Issues	More Facts and Comments

What Do You Think About?

Is the sedation **drug induced**?

Is the sedation due to morphine, other sedative drugs or both?

The **sedative effect** of opioid drugs is normally short-lived. The effect will be aggravated by the concomitant use of other sedative drugs, such as benzodiazepines.

Are there any factors in the patient's clinical condition that are likely to cause sedation, such as uraemia or hypercalcaemia?

Hypercalcaemia should not be considered in isolation. How active the treatment should be in an individual patient will depend on how distressing the symptoms are and whether any further treatment of the malignancy is available.
D Doyle and T F Benton (1991)

What Should You Try To Find Out?

Review any recent investigations, eg serum calcium level.

Review all drugs prescribed for the patient.

Establish as accurately as possible from the patient what their fears of sedation are. Enquire whether they wish to ask you any questions about their future.

The Key Issues	*More Facts and Comments*

What Do You Do?

Where possible, and appropriate, correct any metabolic abnormalities.

While it is frequently not possible to correct the cause of uraemia in a patient with advanced disease, it is often possible to correct hypercalcaemia. Adequate hydration may be sufficient to lower the serum calcium to a level where sedation is not a problem. This, however, will not sustain the process. If the corrected serum calcium is greater than 3 mmol/L, the addition of biphosphonates, e.g. pamidronate in a dose of 15-30 mg as an infusion over two to four hours, will usually be effective. This may need to be repeated after 24 hours and again at intervals of two to three weeks.

Hypercalcaemia should not be considered in isolation. How active the treatment should be in an individual patient will depend on how distressing the symptoms are and whether any further treatment of the malignancy is available.
D Doyle and T F Benton (1991)

Avoid the use of sedative drugs.

Where sedation is required at night, a short-acting **hypnotic** should be used. Centrally acting **anti-emetic drugs,** such as cyclizine and haloperidol, should be avoided. Domperidone, metoclopramide or cisapride could be substituted.

The Key Issues	*More Facts and Comments*

Consider the use of **co-analgesics** for the control of pain.

Consider the use of non-drug measures such as radiotherapy.

Explain any temporary sedative effects of treatment offered and negotiate what you will do if these are too unpleasant.

How Do You Know If You Have Been Effective?
Review the patient daily.

Looking forward

In theory, the needs and wishes of the patient should be paramount in determining what happens in these cases. However, it is right to explore with the patient what lies behind the wish not be sedated.

A13   *The Patient Refuses More Treatment*

The Key Issues	*More Facts and Comments*

What Do You Think About?

Many of the problems related to this issue arise from mistaken beliefs held by the patient or family. Therefore, you need to ponder on the question

- what misunderstanding and **fears** does the patient have about the treatment and stage of the disease?

What Should You Try To Find Out?

Take a careful history from the patient, making it clear that they are not under any obligation to accept any treatment. They should be assured that any likely benefits and side-effects will be honestly explained to them.

The essence of effective communication is in the relationship between the patient and three groups: the caring team, the family and others around the patient. We need to know what the patient is thinking and feeling. We want the patient to know that we shall be available to listen to what he or she wants to say, to allow expression of **fears** and anxieties and to help resolve them.

Another professional who has sufficient knowledge to understand the issues involved, but on whom the patient is not dependent for day-to-day care, has an important role to play here. He or she can listen to the pros and cons, ask pertinent questions, give or obtain more information, and act as a trusted spokesman.
A Stedeford (1984)

The Key Issues	*More Facts and Comments*

What Do You Do?

Review

- the treatment offered to the patient.
- the indications and the need for such treatment.
- the patient's past experience of this treatment, including any information they may have from other sources.

What alternative treatments are available?

Allow the patient to consider all options, giving adequate time for consideration.

How Do You Know If You Have Been Effective?

Allow time for further discussion with the patient and with relatives.

Arrange for the patient to be reviewed by a senior colleague.

The Key Issues	*More Facts and Comments*

Looking forward

The beliefs held by the patient and family are often unfounded, and result from poor communication. This can be avoided by giving a full explanation of the drugs used. Anticipate the common responses, anxieties and misunderstandings. Dispel unrealistic fears about drug tolerance and addiction.

Are there other patients who may not be clear about the plan for their care?

A14   A Different 'Starting Point' for Opioid in Elderly Patients?

The Key Issues	More Facts and Comments
What Do You Think About?	
The patient's general condition other than their chronological age.	Older patients are more likely to suffer from coincident conditions unrelated to their main diagnosis.
The presence of any renal impairment.	Deterioration in renal function is more frequently found in elderly patients. This will affect the clearance of the potent metabolite morphine-6-glucuronide (M-6-G), which contributes significantly to the analgesic effect of repeated oral doses of morphine.
	A highly significant effect of age can be seen with much higher dose requirements in younger patients. The explanation for this is not clear.
Previous exposure to opioid drugs.	*Pharmacokinetic data suggests that disposition of morphine in the elderly is altered with a much smaller volume of distribution which may account to some extent for their lower dose requirements.*
	P J Hoskin and G W Hanks (1988)
What Should You Try To Find Out?	
Results of recent biochemical tests.	
Any likely abnormality, based on their general clinical condition.	

The Key Issues	*More Facts and Comments*

What Do You Do?

Begin with a weak opioid such as codeine or dextropropoxyphene combined with paracetamol (co-proxamol).

If a strong opioid is required, begin with a low dose, such as morphine 2.5 to 5 mg four-hourly, and titrate upwards depending on response.

How Do You Know If You Have Been Effective?

Assess the patient's response to the opioid in terms of pain control.

Review frequently, gradually increasing the dose of opioid until the patient's pain is controlled.

Use the **analgesic ladder.**

The Key Issues	*More Facts and Comments*

What Do You Think About?

What type of movement?

Pain related to weight bearing and movement may herald otherwise undetected **bone metastases.**

What Should You Try To Find Out?

Is the patient free of pain at rest?

What is the cause of the patient's pain? Consider the need for X-rays and bone scan.

Does the patient have **more than one type of pain?**

What drugs are being prescribed?

The Key Issues	*More Facts and Comments*

What Should You Do?

Establish, with the patient, the limits of their mobility

Review the frequency and the timing of all drugs prescribed.

Consider appropriate therapies.

When treating bone pain due to metastases always remember that
- radiotherapy is the treatment of choice
- bone pain often responds well to NSAIDs, especially when combined with opioid drugs.

Set **realistic goals** with the patient.

It is very important to set realistic goals with a patient when their pain is first assessed. The first aim might be to ensure that the patient gets a full night's sleep free of pain. The second goal might be to ensure that they are free of pain at rest and the final goal might be that they can move without pain.

"*It may be necessary for the patient to change their lifestyle and valuable help can be obtained from occupational therapy and physiotherapy colleagues. Splinting or surgical fixation of bones with metastatic deposits will help to relieve pain and has the added advantage of preventing pathological fractures.*"
W M O'Neill, Consultant in Palliative Medicine

The Key Issues	**More Facts and Comments**

Encourage the patient to anticipate pain, to take appropriate doses of appropriate drugs prior to any planned activity (such as an extra dose of morphine, similar to that in **breakthrough pain).**

How Do You Know If You Have Been Effective?

Review the patient regularly.

Looking back

Have you carried out the necessary investigations and consultations prior to your patient developing pain on movement?

Looking forward

What can you anticipate might happen to this patient's pain?

While the basic principle - continuous pain requires continuous therapy - always applies, additional therapy may be necessary prior to any planned activities.

Breakthrough pain - A18

The Key Issues	More Facts and Comments

What Do You Think About?

What is the particular problem?

Have the basic principles of pain control been applied to the problem?

What particular expertise is offered by your local pain clinic?

In various studies, up to 75% of patients, on admission to palliative care units, are suffering from pain. Much of that uncontrolled pain results from a lack of adherence to basic principles of pain control, such as continuous analgesia for continuous pain and the WHO **analgesic ladder**. In some patients, **co-analgesic (adjuvant) drugs** have seldom been used adequately.

The techniques offered by pain relief clinics to cancer patients include:

- percutaneous coeliac plexus block (e.g. in pancreatic and other upper gastro-intestinal malignancies)
- epidural analgesia (e.g. in intractable pelvic pain)
- percutaneous lumbar sympathectomy (e.g. in tenesmus)
- percutaneous cordotomy for unilateral pain.

The Key Issues

What Should You Try To Find Out?

What is the diagnosis of the particular difficult pain problem?

Is the current treatment appropriate? Can it be improved upon?

Is further expertise likely to be of benefit?

Could the administration of drugs by a different route be of benefit, e.g. **epidural opioids?**

Are there any anaesthetic or neurolytic blocks that would be of benefit?

More Facts and Comments

Once the basic principles have been applied, there remains a small percentage of patients, probably less than 5%, who require the expertise of the specialist pain relief clinic.

A further small percentage of patients has pain that is readily controlled with oral analgesics but might be more conveniently controlled with a specific nerve blocking procedure. One example is the use of a coeliac plexus block for pain due to carcinoma of the pancreas.

In a study of 158 consecutive patients admitted to the continuing care unit at the Royal Marsden Hospital in London, only one patient had a coeliac plexus block for pain and nausea resulting from a primary carcinoma of the pancreas.
P J Hoskin and G W Hanks (1988)

The Key Issues	*More Facts and Comments*

What Do You Do?

Refer the patient for assessment. If this is not possible, discuss the problems with the specialists in the local pain relief clinic.

How Do You Know If You Have Been Effective?

Review the treatment offered by the local pain relief clinic and discuss with the patient its likely benefit.

Looking forward

The services offered by the pain relief clinic are invaluable in certain situations. It is important to realise that palliative care and your effectiveness in controlling symptoms, with the aim of improving the quality of the patient's life, depend on the complementary roles of professionals in various fields.

The Key Issues	*More Facts and Comments*

What Do You Think About?

The introduction of the epidural route for the administration of opioids opened up a new era in the treatment of pain. Before using this route, you should think about

- the use of invasive procedures in patients with advanced disease or, in other words, the indication for the use of indwelling epidural catheter

Even when the basic principles for the use of analgesic drugs are adhered to, some patients experience considerable side-effects from systemic opioids. Those patients are likely to benefit from the use of much smaller doses of morphine or diamorphine, injected into the epidural space.

As a starting dose roughly 10% of the oral opioid dose for epidural administration can be used. However, these rules are of no value in cases of patients experiencing insufficient pain relief with oral opioids.
E M Delhaas and J R B J Brouwers (1989)

Opioid drugs administered in this way require the presence of an implanted epidural catheter. This frequently poses problems for patients who might otherwise be cared for at **home**: most community nurses are not trained in the use of epidural catheters and drugs. It may be possible to train the patient or a family member to manage the catheter.

A subcutaneous tunnelled spinal catheter combined with a totally implanted large diameter access port system with a rigid membrane, enhance the likelihood of easy and correct needle insertion even by relatively unskilled people involved in home care.
E M Delhaas and J R B J Brouwers (1989)

- access to a specialist centre
- the care of patients with epidural catheters

The Key Issues	More Facts and Comments

What Should You Try To Find Out?

Can the patient's pain be controlled by simpler methods?

Who will arrange for the insertion of an epidural catheter?

What drugs can be used?

Drugs other than opioids, e.g. local anaesthetics, may be administered epidurally. Occasionally, a combination of an opioid and a local anaesthetic may be beneficial.

Is this method of administration of these drugs likely to be more effective than current treatment?

The progressively higher doses of opioids eventually result in blunting of the psychoemotional sphere in many patients. Under these circumstances some advocate the epidural route because there is little impact on the sensorium.

The best response to epidural morphine is obtained in cases of somatic or visceral pain. Very limited or no response can be achieved in neurogenic pain.
E M Delhaas and J R B J Brouwers (1989)

The Key Issues

More Facts and Comments

Is there any complication of long-term epidural opioid administration?

Fibrosis may occur around the catheter. This is clinically characterised by pain during injection, obstruction, leakage around the catheter and insufficient pain control. Important factors in the prevention of fibrosis formation are: morphine solutions without additives, a pH of about 5 and the choice of the catheter material. Either silicone and polyurethane epidural catheters have been advocated. Delhaas and Brouwers (1989) however, find an unacceptably high incidence (30%) of fibrosis formation with a polyurethane epidural catheter.

Will epidural opioid administration prevent the patient being discharged home if this is their wish?

What Do You Do?

Reassess the patient's pain.

Reassess the treatment offered.

Refer the patient to the **pain relief clinic,** if indicated.

The Key Issues	*More Facts and Comments*

How Do You Know If You Have Been Effective?

Discuss the procedure to be performed with the patient.

Discuss the likely effectiveness with the patient.

Review the patient after the administration of epidural drugs.

Looking back

Was the epidural route, though invasive, fully justified?

Looking forward

Will the facilities available in your hospital, or region, allow the use of this approach in the future?

A18   *The Most Appropriate Use of Syringe Drivers*

The Key Issues	*More Facts and Comments*

What Do You Think About?

Is the patient unable to take medicine by mouth?

The oral route is the best way of taking opioids and other medicines in advanced malignancy. However, this may not be feasible, as in

- persistent **nausea** and **vomiting**
- **dysphagia**
- intestinal obstruction
- profound weakness
- falling conscious level or coma.

Are there alternative routes of drug administration?

Alternative routes

1   *Rectal route*

This should be considered before moving to the next alternative.

2   *Continuous subcutaneous infusion (CSCI)*

Administration of drugs by continuous subcutaneous infusion, via a portable syringe driver or other infusion device, is a valuable option for symptom control.

The Key Issues	*More Facts and Comments*
	Advantages of continuous subcutaneous infusion include • maintenance of plasma concentrations of drugs • avoidance of four-hourly injections - which may be inconvenient, painful and disruptive • maintenance of patient's mobility and independence.

What Should You Try To Find Out?

Assess the patient regarding

• present symptoms
• physical, mental and conscious state
• ability to swallow
• present oral treatment schedules.

The Key Issues	*More Facts and Comments*
What infusion device is available?	A number of suitable devices for continuous subcutaneous infusion are available. It is not possible to give details of them all here. Most are battery operated and may differ in the method of operation, particularly in setting the delivery rate. The Graseby syringe drivers, type MS16A (blue panel) and type MS26 (green panel), are described here because they are widely used in the UK. This does not imply that these two models are any better than the others. It should be noted that syringe drivers are undergoing continual development and improvement. If you are using a different device, please check the instruction booklet supplied with the device and consult with ward staff and the clinical pharmacist. The MS26 has a boost facility to deliver an accurate bolus of medication. Type MS16A is limited to 24 hours only: the MS26 can be set to run for more than one day.

The Key Issues

What Do You Do?

Explain the use of the syringe driver to the patient.

Plan the patient's 24-hour parenteral opioid schedule.

- Use diamorphine in the syringe driver.

  Diamorphine is the opioid of choice in continuous subcutaneous infusion: its high solubility reduces the volume of diluent necessary.

- The 24-hour dose of diamorphine to be administered by the syringe driver is equivalent to one-third of the total oral morphine given to the patient over the 24 hours preceding the use of the syringe driver.

More Facts and Comments

The MS16A (blue) Graseby syringe driver

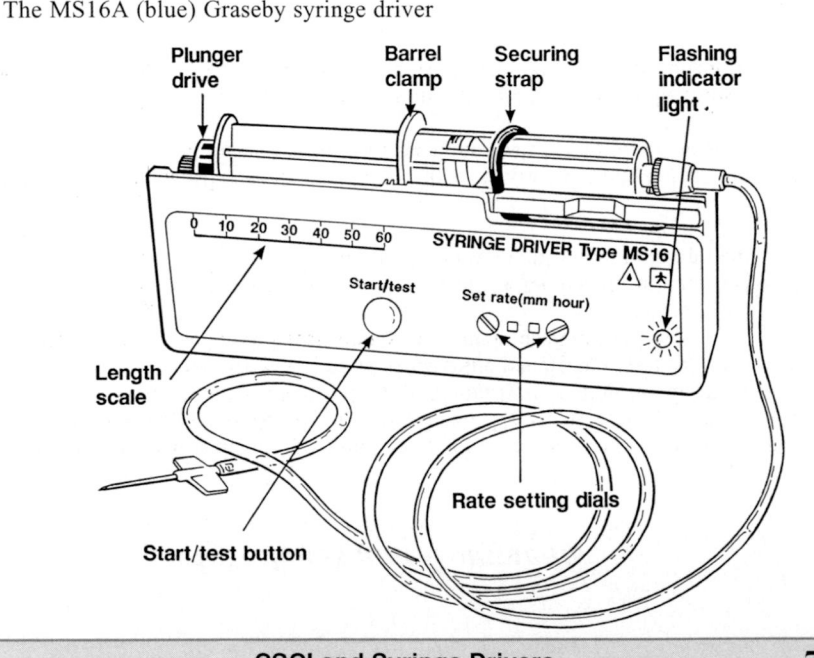

The Key Issues	*More Facts and Comments*

In other words, the 24-hour parenteral dose of diamorphine

= last 24-hour dose of oral morphine
divided by 3.

- Calculate the 24-hour dose of compatible **anti-emetic** and/or **antispasmodic.**

Prepare the syringe driver for action.

- Insert a 9V alkaline battery, e.g. Duracell type MN1604.
- Draw up the required drug solutions to a length of 50 mm, as measured on the scale on the front of the driver.
- Connect syringe to a 100 cm infusion set and use a butterfly cannula (gauge 25) for injection, as recommended by the manufacturer.
- If this is a new infusion, prime the infusion set needle with solution from the syringe.

❝At Roxburghe House we use a 61cm anaesthetic extension set or manometer connecting tube and a 22 gauge Teflon IV cannula for injection. **❞**
J M Leiper, Consultant in Palliative Medicine

Anti-emetics - A19, C6 and C7   Antispasmodics - A19

The Key Issues

- Set rate, using the measuring scale on the syringe driver to measure the distance L that the plunger will travel in millimetres.

MS16A (blue panel)

Set rate = $\dfrac{\text{distance } L \text{ in mm (48)}}{\text{infusion time in hours (24)}}$

= 2mm/hour

MS26 (green panel)

Set rate = $\dfrac{\text{distance } L \text{ in mm (48)}}{\text{infusion time in days (1)}}$

= 48mm/24 hours

More Facts and Comments

Fluid length L in syringe

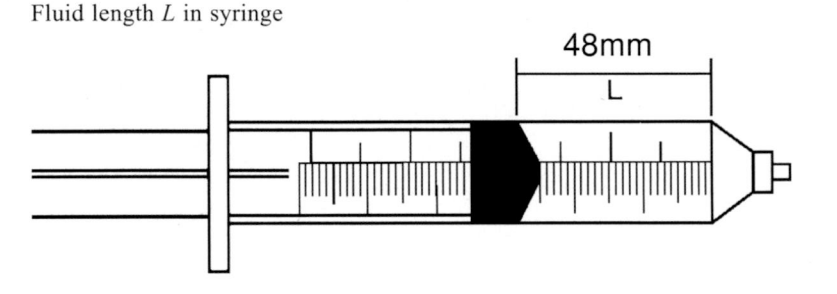

48mm

Always set up a syringe driver to make L about 50 mm with diluent before priming the infusion set. Priming will take about 2 mm of this total, leaving 48 mm of fluid to be transfused over 24 hours. This makes the arithmetic of setting easier.

" *It is best that L is made to equal 48 mm with diluent. The volume this represents is not important. For instance, for a distance L of 48 mm the volume will be bigger in a 20 or 30 ml syringe. The volume also varies from one brand of syringe to another. The dose and the distance L are the important factors not the volume.* "
J M Leiper, Consultant in Palliative Medicine

The Key Issues

- Fit syringe, with infusion set attached, on to syringe driver, using the plunger clamp and the neoprene strap.
- Fit plunger. Release actuator assembly by pressing the white release button. Slide actuator assembly along screw until it fits firmly against syringe plunger. The driver is now ready for use.

Choose an appropriate site for subcutaneous infusion. Insert the needle and secure it with a transparent dressing.

More Facts and Comments

Site selection

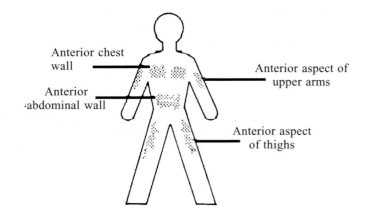

Anterior chest wall

Anterior abdominal wall

Anterior aspect of upper arms

Anterior aspect of thighs

The Key Issues	*More Facts and Comments*
Start the driver by pressing and releasing the start/test button (MS16A) or the start/boost button (MS26).	Remember • if breakthrough dose is used frequently, reassess the prescription before the syringe driver is reloaded. • for breakthrough pain, prescribe one-sixth of the total daily dose of analgesia. Thus, if the syringe driver contains 200 mg diamorphine for 24 hours, the breakthrough dose is 30 mg diamorphine subcutaneously, as required. • **bowel care** is still needed, eg suppositories or enemas. *It is recommended that a loading dose equivalent to a four hourly dose of opioid should be given intramuscularly or subcutaneously as the syringe driver is started. This will avoid any lag period during which adequate blood levels are attained.* *R G Twycross and S A Lack (1984)*
Check site of injection daily for signs of induration and inflammation. The syringe driver can be placed in trouser pocket, shirt pocket, a shoulder holster or in a fashionable 'bum' or waist bag.	

The Key Issues

It is important to
- explain to the patient/relative how the pump works
- reassure the patient of freedom of mobility while on the pump
- consult with hospice staff for advice.

How Do You Know If You Have Been Effective?

Indicators of good performance are
- satisfactory pain control and no breakthrough pain
- satisfactory control of other symptoms
- patient satisfaction
- infusion running to set time
- no leaks
- no signs of skin irritation.

More Facts and Comments

Troubleshooting
This fault-tracing guide for syringe drivers is based on the Graseby types MS16A and MS26.

1   ***Syringe driver will not start***
- No battery.
- Battery inserted the wrong way round.
- Flat battery (alkaline battery usually lasts about three weeks).
- Malfunction of motor.

2   ***Infusion stopped or alarm sounded***
- Empty syringe - actuator at the end of its travel.
- Inflamed injection site.

3   ***Infusion ended early***
- Infusion set primed after fluid length in syringe was measured.
- Incorrect rate calculation and setting.
- Boost button pressed (MS26 model).

4   ***Infusion taking longer than intended time***
- Pump stopped, or has stopped and been restarted.
- Actuator was not flush against the plunger.

The syringe driver has allowed parenteral medication to be continued over longer periods with little discomfort to the patient, but the need still remains for regular and continual reassessment of the patient and his symptoms.
D J Oliver (1988)

A19 *Mixing Drugs in a Syringe Driver*

The Key Issues

What Do You Think About?

Diamorphine may be mixed with other drugs to control more symptoms than pain alone.

Drugs may be incompatible in a syringe driver (e.g. precipitation and crystallisation when mixed at a particular concentration).

How stable are the drugs over the period of infusion (usually 24 hours)?

Drugs should cause neither skin irritation nor subcutaneous inflammation.

More Facts and Comments

Continuous subcutaneous infusion is a method of symptom control that can provide relief of more than one symptom via one route.

Diazepam is not suitable for syringe driver use: it is immiscible with water-soluble drugs and it causes irritation when injected subcutaneously.

Chlorpromazine and prochlorperazine are also not suitable for subcutaneous infusion: they cause skin irritation and the latter breaks down on exposure to light.

The Key Issues	*More Facts and Comments*

What Should You Try To Find Out?

Is there a need for adding other drugs to the opioid?
Examples include

- an anti-emetic

Metoclopramide, cyclizine, haloperidol and methotrimeprazine may be used if an anti-emetic is required. Metoclopramide should be avoided in intestinal obstruction because of its predominantly peripheral action. Cyclizine causes skin irritation in some patients. This can be minimised, or avoided, by changing the site of injection daily or on alternate days. Methotrimeprazine is a particularly effective anti-emetic with a major sedative effect.

We recommend that cyclizine/diamorphine or haloperidol/diamorphine mixtures are not used in slow infusion pumps. These mixtures should be used at low concentrations and infused over a period not longer than 24 hours. Metoclopramide/diamorphine mixtures should be closely observed for signs of degradation. Hyoscine/diamorphine mixtures appear to be stable and thus suitable for use with slow infusion pumps.
C Regnard, S Pashley and F Westrope (1986)

- an antispasmodic for colic
- an anticholinergic for excessive bronchial secretion

Hyoscine hydrobromide and hyoscine butylbromide are anticholinergic drugs with antisecretory and smooth muscle antispasmodic effects. The hydrobromide salt readily crosses the blood/brain barrier and so has central effects. It may cause blurring of vision, sedation and hallucinations.

The Key Issues

- a sedative in the **confused** or **restless patient**

- other drugs.

What Do You Do?

Prescribe the most convenient drug combinations in the proper dose and concentration.

If in doubt, check with the clinical pharmacist, staff of pain clinic or hospice.

Protect syringe contents from exposure to light.

More Facts and Comments

Midazolam is a benzodiazepine which may be administered intravenously or subcutaneously. It is particularly useful in the care of a restless or agitated patient.

Dexamethasone may be administered by subcutaneous infusion or as a single daily subcutaneous injection. It is compatible with diamorphine in an infusion but commonly causes precipitation when used with other drugs.

The Key Issues

How Do You Know If You Have Been Effective?

Assess symptom control, preferably 4-6 hours after commencement, then daily.

Regularly inspect
- site of injection - if inflamed, change site
- syringe contents for change of colour, precipitation, crystallisation
- infusion set - if there is a leak at junction with syringe/ needle, fit a new infusion set.

More Facts and Comments

"It is absolutely essential to check the doses, concentrations and drug interactions before preparing syringe drivers.

To minimise syringe driver reactions, try a small size (22 gauge) IV cannula, e.g. Venflon, subcutaneously instead of a steel cannula but it is important to note that these may kink and interrupt the flow of drug. **"**
J M Leiper, Consultant in Palliative Medicine

A20   *Discontinuing a Subcutaneous Infusion*

The Key Issues	*More Facts and Comments*

What Do You Think About?

Can you discontinue subcutaneous infusion in a patient who has been on a syringe driver for some time?

Think about
- nausea and vomiting - settled?
- dysphagia - settled?
- bowel obstruction - settled?
- confusion/restlessness - improved?
- conscious level - improved?

What Do You Do?

Explain to the patient what you plan to do.

Calculate the equivalent dose of oral morphine to be prescribed as morphine sulphate solution or tablets four-hourly, or sustained-release morphine tablets 12-hourly.

You can discontinue a subcutaneous infusion if the original indications for using it resolve. The sooner the oral route is re-established the better it is for the patient and for symptom control.

"*A syringe driver must not be seen only as a means of prescribing drugs in the last few hours or days of life. It is a useful method of administering drugs when the oral route is, for various reasons, not practical.*"
T F Benton, Consultant in Palliative Medicine

The total dose of oral morphine for the 24 hours following discontinuation of subcutaneous infusion is three times the total parenteral diamorphine for the last 24 hours.

The Key Issues	More Facts and Comments

Prescribe any additive drugs orally.

Observe the patient carefully in the next 12-24 hours to ensure symptoms remain well controlled by oral drugs.

How Do You Know If You Have Been Effective?

Have the patient's symptoms remained under control after the subcutaneous infusion was discontinued?

The Key Issues	More Facts and Comments

What Do You Think About?

The fact that you are responsible for a particular patient should make you aware of their condition and suffering. You should pause to ponder the following issues.

- Is your **assessment of the patient's pain** correct?

Remember the following facts.

- Pain is a major symptom in about two-thirds of patients with advanced cancer.
- We should accept the patient's complaint of pain.
- Pain in advanced cancer can be due to cancer, to a complication of the disease, a side-effect of treatment, or a coincident disease.
- The patient's perception of pain can be altered significantly by pain tolerance, physical condition, anger, depression, anxiety, fear, social and financial loss, the need for more attention, and spiritual unrest. A proper assessment of pain, and its eventual management, must consider all components of **total pain**.

Pain is what the patient says it is and exists when he says it does.
M McCaffery (1983)

" *The pain is all around me!* "
A patient

Pain is!
P D Wall (1977)

" *Pain is a subjective experience. You cannot deny the experience but you may need to diagnose the cause.* "
J M Leiper, Consultant in Palliative Medicine

The Key Issues	*More Facts and Comments*

- Has the problem been clearly defined and presented factually and unemotionally to the senior member of the team?

What Should You Try To Find Out?

Has the patient been seen recently by the senior member of the team?

Has the patient explained the problem to you, nurses or relatives?

Have you explored the patient's insight into diagnosis and prognosis?

Is the patient's reporting of pain consistent?

The use of annotated **pain charts** may clarify the explanation.

Nurses are constantly observing the patient and will have clues to the existence of pain, such as

- reduced activity
- onset of agitation
- local tenderness.

Nerve pain can often be authenticated by its neurological distribution or the presence of other neurological signs.

Pain charts - A5   Nerve damage pain - A9

Pain and the Team

The Key Issues	*More Facts and Comments*

What Do You Do?

Present the problem to the senior member of the team in a coherent non-emotive fashion.

Explore the senior's attitude to analgesia, especially opioids.

Suggest it is not just physical pain.

Suggest a strategy of management to the senior member.

How Do You Know If You Have Been Effective?

Careful attention to the treatment offered will ensure minimal side-effects with maximum benefit.

Ensure the senior member sees the benefit of the treatment regimen.

Contrary to popular belief morphine taken solely to control pain is not addictive. Yet patients worldwide continue to be undertreated and to suffer unnecessary agony.
R Melzack (1990)

A22 *The Ward Team Does Not Believe in Using High Doses of Opioids*

The Key Issues

What Do You Think About?

Which particular member of the team is sceptical?

What influence do they have over other members of the team?

Do they have realistic or unrealistic fears of opioids?

What Should You Try To Find Out?

What are the particular anxieties about the use of opioids?

Has there been some unsatisfactory past experience with opioids?

Are all the team members aware of modern advances in the use of opioids?

Is there a senior member of the team who is familiar with the use of opioids?

More Facts and Comments

There is no fixed dose of morphine for the control of chronic pain. The basic principle of the use of morphine is to begin with a low dose, e.g. 5-10 mg. Administer it regularly every four hours. Increase the dose until the patient's pain is controlled or until side-effects become troublesome. There is no arbitrary upper limit to the dose required.

There has been a move away from the old routine of 'standard' doses given only 'as required'. The dose of opioid should instead be titrated against the pain for each patient until control is achieved. Dose requirements may vary enormously from 30 mg to 1000 mg a day, or much higher doses in some patients.
G W Hanks and R G Twycross (1984)

The Key Issues	*More Facts and Comments*

What Do You Do?

Provide the theoretical evidence in written form, preferably from published work.

If possible present this work or arrange for it to be presented at a clinical meeting attended by the ward team.

How Do You Know If You Have Been Effective?

Create an opportunity for further discussion of the problems.

Looking forward

Learning from experience is always solid and lasting. It also helps a change of attitudes towards a particular line of treatment. When you present clear, documented and well-founded issues to other members of the team, they are more readily accepted.

A23   Colleagues Feel You are Overstating the Patient's Pain

The Key Issues	More Facts and Comments

What Do You Think About?

If you are sure of your factual and objective assessment of the patient's pain, all that you need do is to get your act together to defend your case. Think about

- what is allegedly being overstated?
- why do they feel that it is being overstated?

What Should You Try To Find Out?

Is the patient able to present his or her own story in a non-emotive fashion?

What objective measures of **pain assessment** can be provided?

"Fear of pain is common and this is no less so in health care workers. This fear of pain may present as denial of its existence. *"*
W M O'Neill, Consultant in Palliative Medicine

The Key Issues	*More Facts and Comments*

What Do You Do?

Arrange for the patient to present his or her own history.

Summarise the problem simply, coherently, and cautiously.

Encourage colleagues to take a separate history, and to observe the patient's response to pain and to any treatment.

How Do You Know If You Have Been Effective?

This can be established by allowing time for further discussion and review of the problem.

It is important that any problems are presented in a simple and coherent fashion without the use of emotive language. Dramatic presentations often prompt scepticism in an audience.

Section B - Communication

Section B: Communication - An Overview

Talking With the Patient

- The patient stops talking to you
- Denial
- Depression or sadness
- "Will I get better?"
- "Don't tell the family"
- "I can't go on"

Talking Together About Cancer and Management

- Talking about the diagnosis
- Talking about metastases
- When the tumour is no longer responding to treatment
- "Why is the treatment not working?"
- "Can I sleep with my wife?"

Talking With the Team

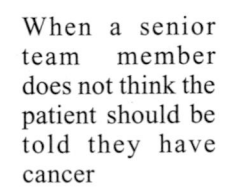

- When a senior team member does not think the patient should be told they have cancer

Talking With the Family

- When relatives are angry
- "Why aren't you controlling the pain?"
- "Why aren't you feeding my wife?"

'Reflections'

- When you feel you are getting too involved
- Distancing
- When you do not have time for relatives

You Need to Tell a Patient That He or She Has Cancer

The Key Issues	*More Facts and Comments*

This may be the first time you've had to talk with a patient about a newly diagnosed malignancy. You may have already watched senior colleagues break **bad news** and gained insight into doctor-patient communication on this issue. However, you may need to identify if you are the best person for this task.

If you need to wait until the 'bad news' stage, the conversation can be difficult. The best preparation for this dialogue is to know your patient. Pick up cues when a patient says, "I'm not looking forward to these tests". Ask a patient before tests: "If the news were bad, what would you want to know, and if you wouldn't want to be told, who would you want us to tell?"

" *Talking to people is not an optional extra.* **"**
Nick Smith, Social Worker

What the doctor tells his cancer patient will depend less on the nature of the illness and personality of the patient, than on his beliefs about divulging information and his own reactions to cancer and death.
I Lichter (1987)

Many patients presenting with symptoms that may signal the presence of a cancer are already worried by that possibility before they visit the doctor.

'Bad news' is any news that materially alters the patient's view of his or her future.
R Buckman (1988)

What Do You Think about?

Bad news can never sound good.

Sharing knowledge with patients does not mean the doctor shares his or her own fears.

The Key Issues	*More Facts and Comments*
Realistic hope should be an essential component of truth telling.	The most important part of the communication is what can and will be done for the patient in terms of the disease. *Uncertainty seems to be the hardest experience of all for the psyche to bear.* *A Stedeford (1984)*
'Telling' involves closely *listening* to the individual patient and identifying their communication needs, their individual fears, their need for 'truth'. What does the patient want to know at this moment?	Without a direct approach from you, many patients never bring themselves to ask questions. Yet, in a brief conversation, they may give clear cues about the information and reassurance wanted. 'Truth' is never black and white. The patient's meaning of 'truth' may differ significantly from the doctor's idea of 'truth'. *'Telling' a patient is only the beginning, certainly not the end.* *A D Weisman (1984)* *Patients are not protected by their ignorance only isolated.* *I Lichter (1987)*
The doctor telling does not mean that the patient understands.	While some patients may remain silent, others may have several questions about the intended plan of management. *Physicians should first encourage patients to discuss their main concerns without interruptions or premature closure.* *Toronto Consensus (1991)*

The Key Issues	More Facts and Comments

What Should You Try to Find Out?

Before meeting the patient

Make sure you know the exact nature of the diagnosis and how the team plans to manage the disease.

Are more tests necessary, e.g. bone scan?

What is the treatment modality: radiotherapy, chemotherapy etc.

Where will this take place?

Are there indicators of how this disease will progress? What are the implications for the life of the patient? How much time may be spent in hospital?

Will the treatment cure or only palliate?

Will the patient experience discomfort or any other symptoms?

Are you the most appropriate person for this task?

• Someone else may have a closer rapport with the patient.

• You may not feel confident to manage this situation, either due to your newness on the ward or to other factors.

The junior doctor may be more aware of the feelings of the patient, more sensitive to his needs and more protective of his rights. However the patient may want to place his trust and confidence with the consultant.
I Lichter (1987)

" *If someone feels inexperienced they can always work initially with another member of the team.* **"**
Nick Smith, Social Worker

The Key Issues	*More Facts and Comments*

The 'climate' for talking about cancer

Find out if other members of the team have insight into how the patient feels. What questions has the patient been asking? What sort of night or morning has the patient had?

Does the patient need some support (friend or relative present) to cope with the news?

Are relatives due to visit today. Will you be able to talk with them later?

What Do You Do?

The beginning

1 Agree with your colleagues the planned strategy.

2 Find a quiet room (somewhere private).

3 Ensure that you will not be interrupted. Check the patient is comfortable.

4 Sit down at eye-level with no barrier between you and the patient.

It can be helpful to discuss the diagnosis with relatives present - but it is important to remember that the news *does* belong to the patient.

"*Problems can occur when patients do not recall information because of their illness. If a relative is present they are able to reinforce what has been said.***"**
K Copp, Macmillan Nurse Teacher

Discussion about prognosis should not include statistical evaluations or too exact predictions about life expectancy.

Do not attempt to deal with the minutiae of complications at this point.

Closed screens around a bed do not always guarantee confidentiality of conversations.

" *The information is the property of the patient and not his relatives. Speaking to relatives first may invite* **"Please don't tell him"** *- which can hinder future communications.* **"**
M Leiper, Consultant in Palliative Medicine

Relatives do not want patient told - B6

The Key Issues

5   Assess the patient's communication needs, i.e. what the patient wants to know.

The following questions may help.

- How do you feel you are getting on?
- What do you feel about your illness?

Listen to the words the patient uses in response to you - 'malignant neoplasm', 'tumour', 'lump' give clues about previous discussions.

More Facts and Comments

66*Its important to check that the patient wishes to talk at this particular time - if not, arrange to come back.*99
Ray Corcoran, Consultant in Palliative Medicine

These open questions are an appropriate way of revealing if the patient
- already has full knowledge of their cancer
- has a suspicion that cancer may be present
- is seeking more information
- is **denying the possibility that they have cancer**
- is completely ignorant that cancer may exist.

66*Be careful: patients may use the words - but don't assume they always understand them.*99
Nick Smith, Social Worker

The Key Issues

6   Decide how much information is appropriate at this point.

The middle

7   Give the news as appropriate...
    Prepare them for bad news.

More Facts and Comments

Patients forget at least 40% of what they hear in an interview and this may be much higher when the news is bad.

The key to breaking bad news is trying to slow down the speed of the transition from a patient's perception of himself as being well to a realisation that he has a life threatening illness.
P Maguire and A Faulkner (1988)

It may be useful to give a warning shot that bad news is to be given, e.g. "Investigations have been completed and the results are not quite as good (or straightforward) as we hoped".

It can be useful to prepare the ground for these discussion at an earlier occasion by using 'What if?' questions, eg:

"What if the news were very bad?"

"If the news were that bad, what would you want to happen, who would be most affected by it?"

"*These questions allow the patients to explore the consequences of bad news without the bad news getting in the way.* **"**
Nick Smith, Social Worker

The Key Issues

Move along the 'bad news staircase', allowing patient/ relative to adjust. Allow frequent pauses to enable 'bad news' to be absorbed.

8   Check for understanding
"Is that clear? Can I answer any queries you have?"
"Would it help if I came back later?"

More Facts and Comments

Avoid jargon.

Give a clear description of the proposed management plan.

Always provide options and leave the patient with hope.

This can often be the point we wish to leave the patient, perhaps feeling relief that the information giving is complete. But beware of this.

There may be a 'shopping list' of queries from the patient. More serious questions may emerge once the patient has had time to think.

Having an understanding of their illness will enable the patient to be part of their management plan.

You need to offer a precise time when you will return and stick to it.

The Key Issues	*More Facts and Comments*

The end

9   Bring the discussion to a close.

Record the conversation in the notes. Tell the nurse on duty about the discussion - so she can be prepared to continue to support the person or answer any queries.

Troubleshooting

The family may wish to control information given to the patient, feeling he or she will 'give up' or be too upset. Their motivation will more than likely be love, a feeling that they want to protect the patient, but

*   the information does belong to the patient
*   explain to the family gently that you have assessed the patient's needs, and you will not withhold the truth when he or she talks about the diagnosis.

The team does need to decide where its responsibilities lie. If the team hasn't discussed the issue team members will be dealing with crises every time.

❝*You don't hand over information about a person's bank account to just anyone, so why do you feel you can do so when it comes to information about their disease?*❞
Nick Smith, Social Worker

❝*If the family wish to control the amount of information the patient receives because they feel the patient will give up, ask them how they know this would happen.*❞
Nick Smith, Social Worker

The Key Issues	*More Facts and Comments*

How Do You Know If You Have Been Effective?

This may be neither easy nor appropriate to measure, immediately after interacting with the patient. It may be more appropriate to reflect on this after the patient has had time to discuss this with the family or time to think themselves. Perhaps the critical criteria are

- meeting the patient's needs,
- the right amount of information,
- given at the most appropriate time,
- with adequate support and time to follow up this conversation, if appropriate.

Looking back

You might like to think about how you carried out this task. Do you feel you could have responded in a different way? What would you do differently? What would you repeat?

Where nothing is hidden, open discussion can occur and the patient is spared the misunderstanding and isolation that ensues when people are afraid to talk.
I Lichter (1987)

"*Hopefully before you have to break bad news to a patient, there has been previous contact. It is during this period that you can establish what sort of detail the patient wants/needs or expects.***"**
Nick Smith, Social Worker

The Key Issues	*More Facts and Comments*

Looking forward

Think how you will continue to support this patient.

Consider making a 'contract' for you or another carer to see the patient later today or on the next day.

Consider how you will support the patient's family and when you will be available to speak to them.

You Need to Explain to a Patient That the Tumour is No Longer Responding to Treatment or That Metastases Have Recurred

The Key Issues	More Facts and Comments

What Do You Think About?

Why do you need to explain this?

- **The patient has asked you about progress.**
- A new, more appropriate, management plan is being considered and the patient needs to be informed.

One of the major grievances voiced by patients is that they were not consulted before treatment was begun and consultation with them about alternative management is even more rare.
S Levin et al (1981)

What is the evidence for the tumour not responding or that metastases have developed? What is the management plan now?

Patients become anxious when treatment plans are altered. They should be informed in advance that it is sometimes necessary to change treatment plans.

What impact will this have on the patient and family, both physically and psychologically?

The occasion of recurrence of the disease may be a time of greater psychological disturbance even than the original diagnosis with findings of more frequently occurring depression and anxiety.
P M Silberfarb et al (1980)

What continuing support will be necessary?

The Key Issues	More Facts and Comments

Remember **bad news** can never sound good.

Sharing knowledge with patients does not mean the doctor shares his or her own fears.

Realistic hope should be an essential component of truth telling, e.g. "We anticipate that we will be able to keep the symptoms under control and you will be at home".

'Telling' involves closely listening to the individual patient and identifying communication needs, i.e. what he or she wants to know at this time.

'Bad news' is any news that materially alters the patient's view of his or her future.
R Buckman (1988)

The most important part of the communication is what can and will be done for the patient in terms of the disease.

Uncertainty seems to be the hardest experience of all for the psyche to bear.
A Stedeford (1984)

Without a direct approach from you, many patients never bring themselves to ask questions. Yet, in a brief conversation, they may give clear cues about the information and reassurance wanted.

'Telling' a patient is only the beginning, certainly not the end.
A D Weisman (1974)

Patients are not protected by their ignorance only isolated.
I Lichter (1987)

The Key Issues

What Should You Try to Find Out?

Before meeting with the patient

Make sure you know exactly how this change in the patient's response to disease will be managed, e.g. will this mean radiotherapy, chemotherapy?

Consult with colleagues who may have a picture of how this patient has responded to change in disease since diagnosis.

Are you the most appropriate person for this task?

- Someone else may have a closer rapport with the patient.
- You may not feel confident to manage this situation, either due to your newness on the ward or to other factors.

More Facts and Comments

Patients may be reluctant to undergo chemotherapy. They may have heard frightening stories of side-effects, such as nausea, general discomfort and hair loss. If radiotherapy is to be given, it should be made clear whether the intent of the therapy is for possible cure, prolonged local control or palliation. The patient needs to be briefed on expected side-effects and reactions.

"*Don't be afraid to involve other members of the multiprofessional team in the telling process.***"**
Nick Smith, Social Worker

The junior doctor may be more aware of the feelings of the patient, more sensitive to his needs and more protective of his rights. However, the patient may want to place his trust and confidence with the consultant.
I Lichter (1987)

The Key Issues	More Facts and Comments

Does the patient need some support (friend or relative present) to cope with the news?

It can be helpful to discuss the management with relatives present - but it is important to remember that the news *does* belong to the patient.

Are relatives due to visit today? Will you be able to talk with them later?

It is an important ethical principle that information is the right of the patient.

The climate for talking

Find out if other members of the team have insight into how the patient feels. What questions has the patient been asking? What sort of night or morning has the patient had?

The fear of recurrence never disappears entirely. People with symptoms are rarely surprised that they have cancer or that it has returned. If a patient has coughed up blood, or seen it in a bowel movement, or has a new pain after cancer surgery, they think of cancer.
I Lichter (1987)

What Do You Do?

The beginning

1   Agree with your colleagues the planned strategy.

2   Find a quiet room (somewhere private).

Closed screens around a bed do not always guarantee confidentiality of conversations.

3   Ensure that you will not be interrupted.

4   Sit down with no barriers at eye-level between you and the patient.

People generally have more trouble with the possibility of cancer than with its discovery or return.
H J Wallace and L A Forti (1978)

The Key Issues	*More Facts and Comments*

5   Assess the patient's communication needs.

"How do you feel you are getting on?"

"What do you feel about your illness?"

These open questions are an appropriate way of revealing if the patient

- has a suspicion that the cancer may not be responding to treatment or has recurred
- is seeking more information
- is denying the possibility that there could be recurrence of problems
- is completely ignorant that a change is occurring in his or her disease status.

The behaviour of cancer is very variable and new situations arise from time to time, often without warning.

The response of the patient to the knowledge that he has cancer also changes and the doctor may find on follow-up that the patient's attitude is now different.

It is mistaken to assume that people either 'want to know' or 'do not want to know'. People vary continuously in what they want to know, how much they want to know and from whom.
I Lichter (1987)

Professionals who rely on a single interview in which to break bad news are likely to find that communication has failed. It saves time to help the patient and his family to come to terms with the realities of illness.
C M Parkes (1978)

The Key Issues	More Facts and Comments

6   Help the patient to decide how much information is appropriate at this point.

You may need to return later to explore further the issues around the change in the disease.

"*Knowledge is power - the object of communication is to allow patients to take control again.***"**
Nick Smith, Social Worker

The middle

7   Give the news as appropriate.

Prepare the patient for bad news.

It may be useful to give a warning shot that bad news is to be given, e.g. "Investigations have been completed and the results are not quite as good (or straightforward) as we hoped."

"*Confirming without being blunt.*

Patient: *"It's not responding to treatment is it?"*
Doctor: *"What do you think?"*
Patient: *"I suppose I knew really."* **"**
Ray Corcoran, Consultant in Palliative Medicine

Avoid jargon.

Give a clear description of the proposed management plan.

Always provide options or leave the patient with hope.

Move along the 'bad news staircase', allowing patient or relative to adjust.

This can often be the point we wish to leave the patient, perhaps relieved that the information giving is complete. But beware of this.

The Key Issues	*More Facts and Comments*
8 Check for understanding. "Is that clear. Can I answer any queries you have?"	Another way to check understanding is rehearsal. Ask patients how they would explain to those close to them, what they have just been told. This also gives you an opportunity to coach them in what might be a difficult thing to explain. Doctor: "Yes, I would find that difficult to understand, why not say..." *It is the right of everyone to make his decisions, whether or not he will undergo any treatment recommended.* *I Lichter (1987)* *It is essential to involve the patient in decision making. Physical dependence does not mean mental impairment.* *I Lichter (1987)*
"Would it help if I came back later?" If the management plan involves new treatment modalities, it is important to obtain informed consent. • The patient must have the capacity to reason and make judgements. • The decision must be made voluntarily without coercion. • The patient must understand his or her right to make choices about the type of care to be received.	You need to offer, and stick to, a precise time when you will return.

The Key Issues	*More Facts and Comments*

The end

9   Bring the discussion to a close.

Record the conversation in the notes. Tell the nurse on duty about the discussion - so she can be prepared to continue to support the person or answer any queries.

It can be useful to look back after you have walked away from a patient. It is often then that facial expression can reveal feelings. It may help to reflect this back to the patient at a later date, e.g. "You looked sad/relieved after I left you last time".

How Do You Know If You Have Been Effective?

You will be in the best position to assess this although communication is a process not merely a one-off intervention.

Do you feel you have answered the patient's questions clearly?

You may wish to use written communications to assist the patient.

'When Cancer Comes Back' is a booklet produced by Cancerlink, available through:

Cancerlink London, 17 Britannia Street, London WC1X 9JN

Tel: 071-833 2451.

This booklet is free to cancer patients.

The Key Issues

Have you achieved informed consent for the next stage of management?

Have you communicated clearly with colleagues throughout this interaction?

Looking back

Reflect on the continuing communication with this patient and on whether the team has a co-ordinated plan.

Looking forward

The challenge is how to provide continuing support appropriately.

- Do involve other colleagues.
- Do be available for the patient and family.
- Do ensure that you can relieve any stress this situation may be triggering in yourself.

More Facts and Comments

If patients are told about their illness early on, the situation does not arise in the terminal stages of the disease where the patient discovers he must lose everything he values.
C M Parkes (1978)

In talking - we must listen. A patient may remain anxious and say nothing or even indicate that he or she has no wish to talk about his or her condition.

With help he may find open discussion is tolerable and his anxiety lessened by venting his fears.

Others who have accepted the inevitability of their death do not wish to be reminded of it. They resent those who keep asking if they would like to talk about it.
I Lichter (1987)

A Senior Team Member Does Not Think the Patient Should be Told He or She Has Advanced Disease

The Key Issues	More Facts and Comments

Do not be too surprised if you find you differ in opinion from your senior colleagues. Such issues provide the challenge of working in a 'team'. Currently, you are the most junior member of the medical team. You work in a hierarchy, so be pragmatic.

Individual doctors strive to protect themselves from assessment and criticism by stressing the uniqueness and uncertainty attached to each case. This serves to support the idea that first-hand experience is the best basis on which to support one's actions.

First-hand experience can be believed to be superior not only to abstract considerations posed in text books but even to general, scientifically verified knowledge.

We may not flinch at telling someone they have heart disease where the prognosis can be very limited, but we will do if the diagnosis is cancer.

" In my view it is iatrogenic cruelty to allow someone to suspect a sinister condition and yet not to have it confirmed or refuted to his satisfaction but to remain in doubt over months or years even in periods of remission. "
D Doyle, Consultant in Palliative Medicine

" The patient may tell you they have advanced disease. "
Frances Sheldon, Social Work Teacher

What do you think about?

Think about your own assessment of the situation. Have you assessed the situation carefully, from the patient and family perspectives as well as from that of your senior colleagues?

Two opposing views

Studies by Oken, 1961, suggested that, in a situation of uncertainty about patient responses, doctors tend to opt for one extreme or another, with the majority believing in and practising the ruling that patients should not be told they have cancer.

The Key Issues	**More Facts and Comments**
	In 1968, 82% of doctors believed they should *not* tell people the truth about their cancers. According to recent surveys, at least 70% of doctors now believe in telling people the truth about their cancers.

What Should You Try to Find Out?

Find out if the patient has been asking question about his or her disease. Ask other team members, nurses, doctors, the social worker.

Find out if relatives have stipulated **the patient is 'not to be told'**.

If relatives have stipulated that the patient is not told, this is an unfortunate and tricky situation. Primarily the relationship is between doctor and patient. If relatives aim to control the situation in this way, it can take time and trust for the doctor to deal with both relatives' fears and patient's needs.
C M Parkes (1978)

What Do You Do?

If you feel the patient is already aware of the seriousness of the disease, or is asking questions of other members of the team, you should explore this issue further.

The Key Issues

Ask the consultant why he or she feels that 'not explaining' is appropriate for this patient. The consultant may feel

- there is evidence of **denial** in the patient or talking with the patient about advanced disease could be potentially harmful
- if such information is shared with the patient, they could **'give up'** and increase the likelihood of psychological morbidity

- not particularly skilled in handling such situations.

Put forward the evidence to support your argument - most of the senior team members will be interested in new information, to help in re-appraisal.

Try to talk through the problem with one of your colleagues.

Accept the final decision of your senior, but continue to raise the issue if it remains important for patient management.

More Facts and Comments

Denial is also a defence mechanism for doctors. I think you have to share your stress with another supportive doctor and be prepared to learn from these experiences.
I Lichter (1987)

Good communication requires honesty and sensitivity.
I Lichter (1987)

The doctor who is ill at ease with cancer and death will engender fear in the patient and in his relatives and friends. He is likely to keep the diagnosis from the patient and avoid other communication with him.
I Lichter (1987)

The patient seems to be denying illness - B10
The patient wants to give up - B15

The Key Issues	*More Facts and Comments*

How Do You Know If You Have Been Effective?

Looking back

Reflect on how this issue arose. Could you have been more aware of the thinking behind some of the management decisions?

Looking forward

Remember that patients still need support and to feel involved, even if there is a limit on the areas you can discuss with them. Be careful you don't find yourself **'distancing'** from patients where the issues are difficult.

Your presentation of issues to the team may well have opened discussion and stimulated others to re-appraise the situation without undermining the authority of your senior.

Patients' communication needs are always changing.

The Key Issues	*More Facts and Comments*

Do make sure, whatever your response is to this issue, that you view it as positive and constructive and make sure you feel well supported by colleagues.

Your priorities for yourself should be

- rest
- relaxation
- re-appraisal.

The Key Issues	*More Facts and Comments*

What Do You Think About?

In general this situation is best avoided, but it can be appropriate

- when you have negotiated with the patient or family that you will do this when information becomes available
- when **relatives** are at a distance and a sudden change has occurred in the patient's condition, e.g. patient is in a Liverpool hospital but relatives live in the Isle of Man.

We will focus on the distant relatives situation.

Given that breaking **bad news** is a complex interaction requiring considerable skill in communication, it is much better handled in a face-to-face meeting. This will allow more support to be given: non-verbal and verbal cues will be better interpreted.

"Breaking bad news over the phone is only one step better than sending the police around - there are few things worse than this. If you can avoid it - don't do it!"
J M Leiper, Consultant in Palliative Medicine

Remember

- bad news can never sound good
- bad news is any news that materially alters the patient's view of his or her future.

The Key Issues

What Should You Try to Find Out?
Make sure that
- you are connected with the right house
- you are speaking to the right person
- the person knows who you are.

What Do You Do?
Make sure you have privacy (e.g. use the duty room). As soon as you know you have the right person, say what you need to say - *simply* and in a *straightforward way*.

Give a warning: "I'm sorry I have some bad news".

Ask them if they are on their own - this conveys concern.

More Facts and Comments

If *serious doubt* exists you can tell them you will phone back immediately having checked the number with directory enquiries.

"News can accidentally be given to the wrong person within the same family - which can merely add to the distress.
J M Leiper, Consultant in Palliative Medicine

"I used to say before I told them: "Have you got someone with you?" or "Are you on your own?" but I always felt they knew what was coming.
Sister in a specialist cancer hospital

The Key Issues	*More Facts and Comments*

Provide the information: "Mr Raleigh died peacefully half an hour ago".

Once you have given then the news, 'be there' for them

- to listen
- to give more information
- to answer questions.

Be prepared to allocate *time* at this stage. You may need to re-organise your work or delegate to someone else.

Continuing support

Ask if there is someone nearby who can support them.

Ask if you can ring someone else for them.

Arrange a time when they can visit the ward - perhaps the following day.

Give your phone number so that they can contact you at a later time if they wish.

The Key Issues	*More Facts and Comments*

How Do You Know If You Have Been Effective?

What you perceive as potential indicators of success may not always be accurate. You are only able to hear the voice on the phone: you cannot interpret other cues. Certainly the 'built-in' option for them to phone you back will have been an indication of support.

Looking back

Could you have planned more effectively for this situation?

You might have been able to discuss with this family what you would do if there was a sudden change in the patient's condition. This could have acted as a warning. It would also identify you as the person who might be talking to them on the phone.

Do you have access to local information, e.g. agencies that the relatives could contact, a stock of booklets suggesting what they can do?

The Key Issues

Looking forward

It will be helpful if you can phone the GP. You can advise if you think the relatives may have particular problems, e.g. with bereavement or with financial issues.

More Facts and Comments

By notifying the GP that the death has occurred and that relatives were informed by phone, you may alert other services that relatives may require support.

"*The number of times I have put my foot in it - by asking a relative how the patient is doing, when they had actually died three or four days before. If only the houseman had phoned and spoken to me or even left a message.***"**
Jim McKellican, GP

B5 *The Patient Does Not Want the Family to Know How Ill He or She is*

The Key Issues

This situation may occur as a specific request from the patient to you not to talk with their family or significant others about changes in their health status. The patient, on the other hand, may merely avoid acknowledging the situation to their family. As when **relatives wish knowledge to be kept from the patient,** it is important to consider the patient and the family together.

What Do You Think About?

You should consider

- the motivation of the patient

More Facts and Comments

'Family' has come to mean more than blood relatives of the patient. It generally stands for the web of relationships that are significant for the patient. Biological links may not be the most important.

*The family is as much the patient as is the dying. Indeed the **stresses upon the family** may exceed those that the patient must bear and he is often more concerned about the emotional state of family members than he is about himself.*
E M Cooperman (1977)

Cancer can sometimes be viewed as an unclean disease, almost shameful.

Denial - the patient may use this as part of denying the seriousness of the disease.

"*The fact that the patient and those close to him are not communicating about the disease can create more barriers than the cancer itself.***"**
Nick Smith, Social Worker

Relatives do not want patient to know - B6
Stressed relatives - B17   Denial - B10   Giving up - B15

The Key Issues	*More Facts and Comments*
• the effect on family interaction • the rights of the patient to have his or her wishes adhered to.	Closed communication within the family can have extensive effects on all parties, generating misunderstanding and isolation. Certainly it is the patient's right that details of disease should remain confidential. However, it is important to discuss the effects of this on both the patient and the family. Normal family development can be pictured as following a pattern which alternates between imbalance and struggle on the one hand and successful adaption on the other. Each of us holds prejudices about what qualities together to make up the normal coping family. These are probably based on our own experience of family. We must be careful these prejudices do not colour our assessment of the situation. *The availability of the doctor on a casual basis may be preferred to regular interviews to report progress; formal meetings are often looked forward to with apprehension, so that much of what is said is not 'heard'.* *I Lichter (1987)*

| **The Key Issues** | **More Facts and Comments** |

What Should You Try to Find Out?

What is the current relationship between the patient and his or her family?

How have both the patient and family previously coped with crises?

How are other members of the team dealing with this situation, or how do they feel it would be useful to act in this case?

Are there other factors to be considered, e.g. the financial implications: "How will they cope if I die?"

It is important to accept that over time the experience may change. You can then explore the consequences with the patient, e.g.

> "How do you think that would affect your family? How are the family at present? What would happen if they did know what was wrong with you? Do you think that they could cope? How have they coped in the past?"

If the answer is "Not well," then ask:

> "Do you think the current situation is the same?"

If the answer is 'Yes', then ask:

> "Is the current situation exactly the same? What strengths might they have gained in the meantime?"

It is possible that some people cannot cope with news about how ill their relative is, but this is often less likely than is feared.
I Lichter (1987)

" *Exploring the consequences of their disease both for the patient and those closest to him, will either clarify and mitigate the potential effects of the disease or make it seem less dangerous to talk openly.* **"**
Nick Smith, Social Worker

The Key Issues

What Do You Do?

There are several options.

- Involve members of the team who may have a closer relationship with this patient and family, e.g. another doctor, the social worker, the ward sister

- agree with the patient and not discuss the situation with the relatives at this time

- provide continuing support with discussion about how this decision affects the patient's isolation and that of the family

- discuss the situation with colleagues to agree a strategy for action.

More Facts and Comments

I The Fireman's Response - the need to be helpful and do something

2 Rescued - everyone feels better

| *The Key Issues* | *More Facts and Comments* |

How Do You Know If You Have Been Effective?

This may only be measured by how well you are enabling the patient to adjust to health status changes and to begin to communicate with the family.

Looking back

It is good that the patient felt sufficiently 'in control' to ask that the family not be informed. However, how had the family originally been helped to cope with changes (test results, treatment, etc)?

Looking forward

It may be that your relationship with this patient and family will require more than a one-off response to a problem. Don't get trapped in the 'rescuer role'. A continuing relationship will be an integral part of successfully resolving any anxieties in the patient or the family.

3   Rescuer's Dilemma - part of the solution or part of the problem?

4   Empowering the Family - planning for making the professional less central.

The Key Issues	*More Facts and Comments*

Collusion is probably the most common problem in early stages of disease diagnosis. Don't feel too frustrated. The dynamics of families change and often very strong emotions are released around the point of diagnosis.

A normal response for people who are close is to try to protect each other from further hurt and suffering. In an effort to give the patient a break and "help them get their strength back", well-meaning members of the family can isolate the patient. This detaches them from previous roles in the family, removing much of the pattern of activity which gave meaning to the patient's life.

*It might start with an anxious husband bullying doctors and nurses into not letting his wife know exactly what is wrong with her. "**She would give up**, doctor, if she knew". But how often do the couple communicate with third parties about what is happening? The pain of talking together is too great.*
Nick Smith, Social Worker

What Do You Think About?

Information is the right of the patient - it is his or her disease.

The family may feel the patient, particularly if elderly or debilitated, would not cope with bad news.

Protection often takes the form of withholding information that may cause pain. A conspiracy ensues, which is difficult to maintain. The family may repress their *own* grief to present a controlled front. This causes severe tension, which drives people who love each other further apart.

Patient wants to give up - B15
Relatives ask why treatment is not working - B20

The Key Issues	More Facts and Comments

The family may feel that, if they deny the problem, it could perhaps go away.

Beware of failure to share information, to communicate both with the patient and the family.

What Should You Try To Find Out?

What do the relatives feel or fear will happen if the patient were aware of his or her disease?

Has the family previously had a bad experience where a relative has died?

Has this family been given special instructions by the patient, e.g. that he or she would not wish to be told?

Do other members of the team have more information?

The Key Issues	*More Facts and Comments*
What Do You Do?	Conversations with different members of staff may well provide the basis for an assessment of whether the patient does or does not know.
Talk with colleagues, nursing staff, the medical social worker, to check their understanding of the situation.	
Agree a plan or strategy. Avoid giving overlapping or conflicting opinions.	
Talk with the family to clarify why they feel this way.	"How would you know if the patient did know the diagnosis? How do you know the patient does not know?"
Explore some of the issues that can influence the patient's experience.	Patients can often guess their diagnosis and feel isolated, needing their suspicions confirmed.
	Sometimes the patient's imaginings can be worse than the actual diagnosis. By opening up fears and anxieties, they can be confronted and resolved.
Explore some of the issues from the relatives' perspective.	Relatives may be communicating non-verbally already. When we feel uncomfortable in a situation, e.g. telling lies, our eye contact, or lack of it, gives us away.
	Relatives can often feel guilt during the bereavement, if barriers have existed during the final part of life.
	The motive will probably be one of love - 'to protect the patient' - but collusion can cause a barrier.

The Key Issues

In summary

The nature of your relationship and interaction with the relatives should promote a trusting environment.

This is essential in supporting patient and family, *but* it is also important to clarify your responsibility to the patient. Say to relatives that

- information will not be inappropriately blurted out
- all of the patient's questions will be answered honestly and every query explored
- you will take your cues, e.g. on amount, nature and pacing of information, from the patient.

How Do You Know If You Have Been Effective?

Does the family still feel well supported, part of the caring team?

Do you still have a good dialogue with family members, without compromising your relationship with the patient?

More Facts and Comments

It is important to establish ground rules.

- You will always tell the truth if asked.
- You will not tell if the patient does not want to hear.
- You will always have the patient as your primary concern.

As with any other phase of the illness, the patient relates to various groups apart from the family. It is all too possible for professionals to become entangled in what should be family business.

The Key Issues	*More Facts and Comments*

Looking back

Can you see any point where earlier information to, or discussions with, the family would have eased this situation?

Looking forward

How can you best help the family on a continuing basis? Consider

- more frequent discussions
- involving them more in planning to provide care for the patient.

B7 *The Patient Asks You Why the Treatment is Not Working*

The Key Issues	More Facts and Comments

What Do You Think About?

Consider

- previous conversations with the patient
- patient's treatment to date
- current status of disease, future plans.

Obtain the management plan and any potential alternatives.

Communication is not dispensed once, then put away. It requires a continuing update, review and reinforcement.

What Should You Try To Find Out?

How does the patient perceive the problem? What indicators are there of recurrence? What changes are there in discomfort, fatigue or weakness as a result of therapy? How does this affect the patient's view of his or her future?

The patient is not faced with one massive loss but with a series of disappointments, each of which he has to deal with before being confronted with the next.
I Lichter (1987)

What Do You Do?

1 Ask the patient what they would like to know.
2 Review management plan with patient.
3 Discuss future options with patient.

The Key Issues

4   Offer to speak with patient and family together.
5   Inform colleagues and record conversation in case notes.

How Do You Know If You Have Been Effective?

Looking back

Were discussions with the patient always open and involving him or her in planning?

Could the patient have been prepared more effectively for limited success of treatment?

Looking forward

Patient and family remain happy to ask questions and explore issues with you.

Planning will achieve a more co-ordinated approach in the health-care team.

More Facts and Comments

The Patient Asks You "Do you think I'll get home?"

The Key Issues	*More Facts and Comments*

Often such questions are mechanisms the patient uses to begin a discussion about the future. Do not fall into the trap of premature reassurance: "Of course you will".

What Do You Think About?

Why is the patient asking this now, e.g. in the middle of your conversation about treatment, as an opening question to get your attention, after having bad news of change in treatment?

How is the patient asking the question, e.g. anxiously or calmly?

What is the patient's need, e.g. reassurance or an opportunity to talk?

The patient will decide if he feels safe enough to discuss his fears with a member of the medical team.
R G Twycross (1987)

The Key Issues	More Facts and Comments

What Should You Try to Find Out?

When questions like this are asked directly, you often have to think on your feet - there is no time to prepare, you cannot find out what other professionals said. But you can find out the most important issues directly from the patient.

- What is the patient's perspective?
- What are the communication needs?

What Do You Do?

Assess carefully what the patient wants to know.

Respond to the issues raised by the patient:
- avoid premature reassurance
- arrange to return later if not all of the questions can be answered at this point
- talk about having a discussion with the family
- speak to family about a home visit if it is not possible for patient to go home for an extended period.

Ask open questions, such as:

"What do you think about getting home?"

"What did Dr A, or Mr B, say about the plan of management?"

"You sound a bit concerned. Can you tell me what's been happening?"

The Key Issues	More Facts and Comments

How Do You Know If You Have Been Effective?

Looking back

You were obviously trusted by the patient. You could review the opportunities that had been made for the patient to discuss any anxieties.

Looking forward

You have the opportunity to advise other members of the team about the continuing communication needs of the patient.

Patients may wish to discuss their disease and change in health status. They may ask when they will be discharged from hospital, or how they will manage at home. However, many patients will ask such questions when their awareness changes. It is not always easy to anticipate when this change will happen.

The Key Issues	More Facts and Comments

What Do You Think About?

Usually patients needing honest answers will ask professionals they trust. There are really three key issues here

- the patient's anxiety about the **dyspnoea**
- the patient's need to talk about how they might die and also when
- the potential need to review the current management of dyspnoea.

What Should You Try To Find Out?

You will need to establish

- the patient's experience of dyspnoea - how often it is occurring, what it means to the patient (e.g. heralding deterioration of condition) and how he or she is currently coping with these issues.
- the patient's need to talk about how he or she might die (now may not be the time, but you will need to assess this).

The patient will decide whether he or she feels 'safe' enough to discuss his fears with a member of the medical team.

Dyspnoea must be one of the worst symptoms a patient can suffer. The sensation of being unable to breathe adequately will generate tremendous fear and panic. I Finlay (1991)

"Tell me about these breathless attacks."

"*Fear is often more to do with the 'how' of dying than the existential fear of death itself.*"
Kate Copp, Macmillan Nurse Teacher

More than a fear of death, the dying fear lonely suffering. Closeness and warmth are appropriate remedies.
A D Weisman (1974)

The Key Issues	More Facts and Comments

- the current problem of dyspnoea, e.g. changes in baseline observations, cough, pleuritic pain and changes in sputum volume and colour.
- the cause, e.g. reactive bronchospasm, tumour invasion of main bronchi, pleural effusion, infection.

Many people have no experience of death and a clear and truthful explanation of what to expect will remove many unrealistic fears about dying.
E Charles-Edwards (1983)

What Do You Do?

The patient does need to feel that you have the time and the interest to discuss these issues, so do respond immediately - it will have taken courage to ask you.

Do not offer premature reassurance, e.g: "Of course you won't - we'll keep everything under control."

"Frequently we cannot give the reassurances we would like and sometimes there is the risk of a very distressing death.
William O'Neill, Consultant in Palliative Medicine

Plan to explore the patient's perception of their dyspnoea and disease.

Review the management - involve colleagues, the family.

The Key Issues	*More Facts and Comments*

How Do You Know If You Have Been Effective?

Looking back

Have you been monitoring physical changes?

Have you been available to talk with the patient?

Looking forward

Will you be able to monitor the severity of the experience of dyspnoea and relieve accordingly any fear about dying?

The Key Issues

What Do You Think About?

Denial is a primitive defence mechanism and enables individuals to cope with very distressing events or thoughts.

What Should You Try To Find Out?

Find out if the denial is healthy or unhealthy.

More Facts and Comments

The initial response of denial is likely to be temporary, or only part of a continually changing picture. At times the patient will seem to know, at others he or she will speak and behave as though they do not.

The fact that a patient makes plans or declines to talk about his illness does not mean that he does not know about or does not accept its nature. It may mean he elects not to dwell on it.
I Lichter (1987)

Healthy denial

- Allows the person to manage unwelcome situations they cannot change, e.g. a person denies they are losing weight as cachexia advances.
- Helps the person to adjust to conflicting ideas that create dissonance or discomfort, e.g. "I'll beat this tumour yet."
- Gives the person time to become accustomed to a major loss before responding to the pain of the situation, e.g. a denial can be a natural response to the death of a loved one.

❝❝*You need to find out what it is that the patient is postponing.*❞❞
Nick Smith, Social Worker

Should you ever force a patient through denial? - B11
Bad News - B1

Feelings and Relationships

The Key Issues

More Facts and Comments

Unhealthy denial

- A reaction that acts as a barrier and prevents the person adjusting to a new situation.

In some situations, if a patient is close to death, it may be unrealistic to expect him or her to face death totally.

Accept that denial has a protective function.

It may be useful to try to 'think into' the situation, to see what feelings and issues the person is avoiding.

How long has this been present?

Who has observed it?

Why is it present?

What is the impact of denial on the person and their family?

Denial should not be reinforced or confronted by your intervention. It is important that patients come to terms with illness in their own way. Rarely reinforcement has a positive role, e.g. when it is obvious that the patient's death is imminent, yet they firmly believe their health is improving. Such occasions need to be part of a carefully planned strategy.

The Key Issues	*More Facts and Comments*

Find out from the team.

- Do they all feel it is denial?
- Are team members aware of how their colleagues are responding?
- Is there a co-ordinated plan?

If you don't have a co-ordinated plan, you could all be responding to this patient and the relatives in different ways - which could cause more problems. You may wish to ask for specialist help, e.g. someone in the local hospice.

What Do You Do?

Discover which professional has the closest relationship with the patient.

It may be that this patient already had a dialogue with another professional. This could be the most appropriate person for them to talk with.

Assess the nature of the denial. Establish whether you are the person to talk with the patient and relatives on behalf of the team.

Explore the issues the person is avoiding.

Give the person an opportunity to discuss his or her beliefs and values.

The Key Issues

Decide whether this is healthy or unhealthy denial.

If denial is healthy, devise your plan as a team - this may mean no intervention, no reinforcement, no confrontation.

If denial is unhealthy - explore how confrontational strategies may enable the individual to come to terms with the situation.

Record outcome and inform colleagues so the team knows how to respond.

More Facts and Comments

❝*Use **'What if ...' questions.** These allow a person to think through and respond to a 'hypothetical problem'. (see B1)*❞
Nick Smith, Social Worker

This may be rare, e.g. a husband denying the seriousness of his illness and causing disruption of the marital relationship and distress to the family. This may result in a lack of planning, for his future care as well as in provision for the family after death. The question is one of priorities and raises the issue of 'family palliative care', i.e. your role in the prevention of distress to others.

'Help the Hospices' have produced a video, 'Promoting Openness', which looks at this issue.

Help the Hospices
34-44 Britannia Street
London   WC1X 9JJ

Telephone: 071 278 5668

The Key Issues	*More Facts and Comments*
### *How Do You Know If You Have Been Effective?*	
It can be an uncomfortable experience, being part of a team looking after a patient in denial.	
You may feel that, initially, conversations are less open than would be healthy.	At a later stage, denial may be shown by failure to comply with the doctor's advice or to plan realistically for the family - the family may suffer considerable anguish as a consequence.
There may also be differences of opinion within the team, or pressure from relatives to force the patient to accept what is happening.	
To be effective, you must carefully plan your interventions. You must also understand and accept the feelings that emerge.	

The Key Issues	*More Facts and Comments*

Looking back

Have you reassessed this patient's physical status? Pain and other symptoms may be interfering with emotional state. Have you talked with the relatives lately?

Looking forward

How best can you support this patient and family?

B11   *Should You Ever Force a Patient through Denial?*

The Key Issues

More Facts and Comments

What Do You Think About?

Remember **denial** is often a healthy defence mechanism. Patients are not usually at a fixed point in their understanding. Sometimes, patients 'know' and are prepared to talk about their situation, illness or death: at other times, they 'don't know'.

When is it *not* appropriate for the patient to remain in denial? Continued denial is inappropriate when someone vulnerable is dependent upon the patient, e.g.

- a young child
- someone with mental health problems
- someone elderly or demented.

"They can say the words, yet not look you in the eye."
Frances Sheldon, Social Work Teacher

The patient does have the right to self-determination and can therefore choose to deny the situation.

These patients can show evidence of severe anxiety while claiming that there is little wrong with them. It is clear that the psychological mechanism which should be reducing their suffering is causing extra difficulty.
I Lichter (1987)

No defence mechanism is maladaptive unless its persistence becomes harmful, causing additional suffering to patient, family and carers.

Denial may have to be confronted when

- the patient using this defence mechanism is not coping successfully
- it is so exaggerated that it isolates the patient from family and friends
- it endangers the patient's best interests or treatment.

The Key Issues	*More Facts and Comments*

What Should You Try To Find Out?

What is the effect of this denial on the family?

The family may be relieved that they do not have to talk with the patient about the illness or death - which can be extremely distressing for them. However, they may be anxious that the patient is not facing up to the situation, being in 'cloud-cuckoo-land'.

> **"** *Not every family is able to be open, loving and supportive in the face of serious illness and death. Latent problems may emerge.* **"**
> *Frances Sheldon, Social Work Teacher*

What does the patient really think? This provides the patient with an opportunity to talk.

It is essential to provide opportunities for patients to talk openly about their perception of the situation.

Are there vulnerable or dependent relatives or significant others in the picture?

What do other members of the team think is happening? Ask the senior registrar or ward sister.

What Do You Do?

Decide with other members of the team how best to co-ordinate your care and whether confrontation is appropriate.

The Key Issues

Offer the patient repeat opportunities to ask fuller questions
  "How do you think things are going now?"
  "Anything worrying you?"

If it is agreed that, for the sake of vulnerable dependants, this patient needs to have their denial challenged, great care must be taken in planning to break the **bad news** and in providing follow-up support.

It is essential that all communication be recorded so that the team can be aware of what is happening with this patient and the family.

More Facts and Comments

Some hospices have a special information sheet that records significant conversations with the patient and uses direct quotes to improve the team's understanding.

"*The key thing I learned from this case was the importance of keeping a written record of conversations - we didn't know what had been said.* "
House Officer

The Key Issues	*More Facts and Comments*

How Do You Know If You Have Been Effective?

With no vulnerable relatives, the patient remains in control and in denial. You may feel uncomfortable, but the patient still talks to you openly.

If you agreed as a team that confrontation was appropriate, effectiveness is indicated by

- reduced anxiety in the patient
- more open dialogue within the family
- more realistic planning/provision made for the future by the patient.

Looking back

It may be useful to reflect on how the situation was managed. Are there learning issues for the team?

Looking forward

Continued monitoring will be necessary. Patient and family will probably continue to need support and opportunities to discuss problems.

B12   *You are Getting Too Involved with a Patient*

<table>
<tr><td>The Key Issues</td><td>More Facts and Comments</td></tr>
</table>

The Key Issues

What Do You Think About?

What does 'too involved' mean? This will depend on you and your relationship patterns. Remember: what is too close for some, is too distant for others.

Think carefully about your own practices. Ask yourself what it is about you or your past experiences that have made you feel so close to this particular patient.

Think about what you understand by professionalism. Do you associate this with having no emotional attachment towards your patients? How can you balance professionalism with interpersonal care?

Think about your own need to be needed.

More Facts and Comments

"To stay useful you have to tread a narrow line between over and under involvement."
Frances Sheldon, Social Work Teacher

Sometimes, a patient reminds you of a member of your family or of a past bereavement.

The Key Issues	*More Facts and Comments*
What Should You Try To Find Out?	
Is it just you, or are other members of the team also 'too' involved?	
How much of this 'attachment' is felt just by you, how much by the patient?	
What Do You Do?	
Do try to keep to your normal working hours.	
Do take breaks.	
Do ask for peer support.	
Discuss the case with another colleague.	
Be open with the patient.	Explain that you feel here is a difference in the tone of your relationship. Say: "I don't think any the less of you, but I feel I'm overwhelmed and need to take a step back."

The Key Issues	*More Facts and Comments*

Ensure that if you do 'step back', other members of the team are told. In particular, one other member of the team should be advised about the situation and prepared to support the patient.

How Do You Know If You Have Been Effective?

You have been effective, if

- . you feel less overwhelmed by your involvement
- . you have gained more insight into why this had been a problem for you.
- . the patient does not feel rejected
- . both you and the patient are supported by your understanding colleagues.

The Key Issues	More Facts and Comments

What Do You Think About?

You may be finding every reason not to go and see one particular patient. You may be delaying interaction with him or her. Think about the meaning of distancing - this will depend on you and your relationship patterns. Think about your own practice. Ask yourself what it is about you, or your past experiences, that makes it difficult to interact with this patient.

What is your usual 'distance' from patients? Is your usual distance the right one? (Each team member has a distance that is right for them.) For some, to have eye contact would be too little: for others, it would be too much to put their arm round a patient. You must find your own comfortable distance.

Staying close to pain in patients and relatives can be very difficult. Vachon calls this effect 'battle fatigue' - the price you pay for **getting close.**

"It was an insidious feeling. I just knew that I didn't feel comfortable with this patient and I kept our time together to a minimum."
A Doctor

"If talking about death and dying makes us feel uncomfortable or embarrasses us, it's hardly surprising if we distance ourselves from dying patients."
Kate Copp, Macmillan Nurse Teacher

"Why do the doctors not talk to me? Why do they just stand at the bottom of my bed?"
A Patient

Those caring for the cancer patient may unwittingly use techniques which keep him at an emotional distance - jollying the patient along, telling him that there is no reason to be upset. Tone of voice, demeanour, facial expression are all ways in which staff unconsciously tell patients that they do not wish to listen to them.
I Lichter (1987)

The Key Issues	More Facts and Comments

What Should You Try To Find Out?

Ask other members of the team what effect this patient is having on them.

What Do You Do?

Acknowledge that there is a problem.

Ensure that you are getting adequate support from colleagues. Take adequate rest/relaxation.

Enable another member of the team to take over for a while.

How Do You Know If You Have Been Effective?

Your actions/feelings do not generalise to other patients.

You find yourself more able to make contact with this particular patient.

You feel better supported by colleagues.

Three possible reasons for distancing are

- fear that the result of interacting with patients would be their release of emotional energy in the form of crying or shouting.
- anxiety about not being able to answer difficult questions.
- avoidance of thoughts of own mortality.

The Key Issues	*More Facts and Comments*

What Do You Think About?

Has there been a change in the patient's physical circumstances?   For example

- pain has increased
- increase in fatigue or other symptoms.

Has there been a change in the patient's personal circumstances? For example

- the relationship between you and the patient may be changing (you have less time; you seem less forthcoming; something happened in a recent interaction).
- the patient may feel there is **no point in going on.**

Don't ignore the possibility that the patient may be unable to talk.

The patient who doesn't talk to you may be giving you a message - it's almost the final means of communication to withhold speech.

They may be saying - "I'm really angry" or "I'm in a gloom".

❝*Your role is to offer your skills to a patient, but it is his choice whether or not he uses them.* ❞
Frances Sheldon, Social Work Teacher

❝*We rely so much on the dialogue between ourselves and our patients that when someone refuses to start one or discontinues one, as professionals, we are lost and feel impotent.* ❞
Frances Sheldon, Social Work Teacher

The patient wants to give up - B15   Denial - B10

Feelings and Relationships

The Key Issues

What Should You Try To Find Out?

Are there any other changes? Ask the staff. Is it only you that the patient is not talking to? Is he or she not talking to other family members or other team members?

Does the patient agree that something has changed?

Remember

If a patient stops talking, it is not necessarily a criticism of you. It may relate to their understanding of illness.

What Do You Do?

Give a clear explanation - to patient and to the family. Do not make relatives feel you are brushing this off. Speak to the social worker, charge nurse. Come back to the patient again. Continue your relationship.

More Facts and Comments

The Key Issues	*More Facts and Comments*

How Do You Know If You Have Been Effective?

You maintain your contact with patient and family.

You gain insight into how the family functions.

The team is able to use your insights to decide a co-ordinated plan of management for the patient and family.

The patient is not ignored.

B15 *The Patient Wants to Give Up*

The Key Issues	More Facts and Comments

This may be called 'turning one's face to the wall'.

Some patients express verbally, or in other ways, that they have had enough treatment, enough chemotherapy. They do not want any more tablets and they may be refusing food.

What Do You Think About?

Quantity versus quality of life.

Patient's rights in determining own treatment.

Your response.

"If the patient's reaction to dying is one of depression, how much can we do to alter that? We may only be able to change things with cognitive therapy. "
Kate Copp, Macmillan Nurse Teacher

It may well be that the patient's current experience has become too painful or too distressing.

The patient may feel out of control - with little choice in how his or her management plan is being decided.

Working with patients who wish to 'give up' or are determined to refuse treatment can make you feel impotent or very frustrated.

"There really is no 'right way to die'"
Kate Copp, Macmillan Nurse Teacher

The Key Issues	*More Facts and Comments*

What Should You Try To Find Out?

Are there physical changes causing this response? For example, has pain experience changed and are symptoms **'out of control'**?

Is the patient **depressed** or **sad**?

What is the patient's understanding of the current situation?

How has this patient responded to previous changes in condition?

Ask relatives how they feel the patient is coping.

Ask the opinion of other members of the team about changes in the patient.

Some patients cope by being helpless. You may find that this behaviour is part of the way the patient has coped previously.

"*Perhaps the patient wants you to say "Don't give up."***"**
Kate Copp, Macmillan Nurse Teacher

Depression and sadness - C23   Pain out of control - A6

Feelings and Relationships

The Key Issues

What Do You Do?

Your response needs to be comprehensive. Involve the perceptions of all the team, who are managing any changes in physical state, but also review the patient's needs.

Those needs include
- the need to be at home
- the need to stop chemotherapy
- the need to talk about fears for the future.

This will require careful negotiation, both with the patient and the family. A planned team response will also be necessary.

Reaffirm the patient's right to choose.

More Facts and Comments

If depression underpins the decision to give up, drug intervention, in addition to support, may be appropriate.

The Key Issues	**More Facts and Comments**

How Do You Know If You Have Been Effective?

Looking back

Review the patient's desire to give up, discover if there were indicators that the patient's physical symptoms were not being adequately controlled. Was there an open dialogue with this patient and family?

Looking forward

It will be essential to continue support, both for the patient and the family. It may well be that the desire to give up heralds a new awareness about dying.

The Relatives are Angry

The Key Issues

More Facts and Comments

Do not be surprised or upset. Anger is a form of expression. This may not seem to you to be the most appropriate time or place for its expression. But anger is a *real* feeling.

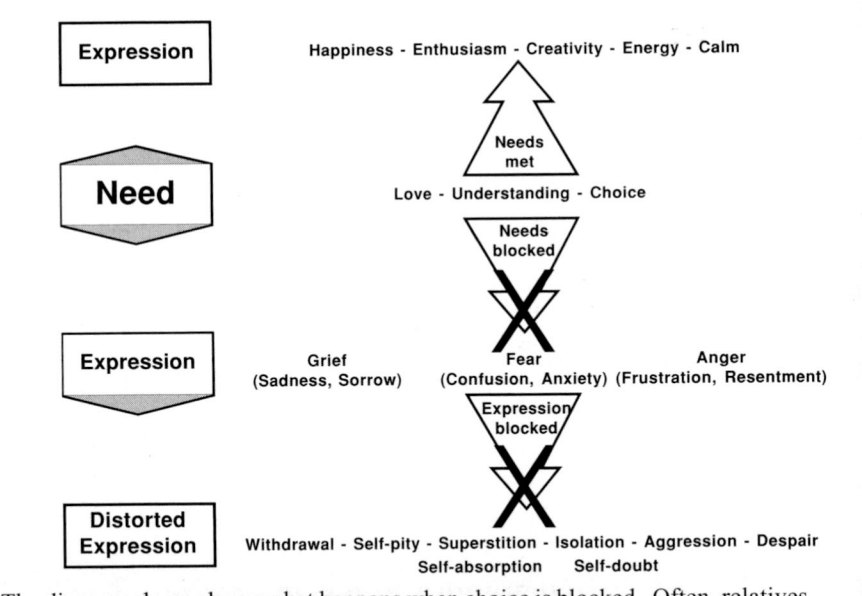

The diagram above shows what happens when choice is blocked. Often, relatives and the patient feel they are forced into a position, that they have no say in deciding about management.

| *The Key Issues* | *More Facts and Comments* |

What Do You Think About?

Relatives can be angry for many reasons.

Anger at members of staff:

- lack of information
- misunderstandings about management
- inadequate pain or symptom control in the patient
- adjusting to bad news or recognition of changing status of patient
- someone, they feel, has given inaccurate information.

"*I think anger is a primitive response and goes back to something most people don't have any control over.*"
Gill Oliver, Regional Nurse Cancer Services

"*Anger can also be seen as a symptom of underlying dis-ease and pain.*"
Kate Copp, Macmillan Nurse Teacher

"*The anger may be justified and reasonable and may be the result of deficits in care provided.*"
William O'Neill, Consultant in Palliative Medicine

"*I think staff may be surprised at how anger in others can affect them. It is important not to feel guilty if angry relatives make you feel angry as well.*"
Gill Oliver, Regional Nurse Cancer Services

The Key Issues	*More Facts and Comments*

Anger at self.
- Guilt because they are not managing patient at home.
- Frustration because they feel they have no control over the situation.

Anger at patient.
- He or she is "leaving the relative".

Anger at other family members.
- Previous family problems.

Anger at the situation itself.
- The dying process over which they have no control.

" *Don't forget if one professional bears the brunt of an angry outburst - then you will need to support them as well.* **"**
Gill Oliver, Regional Nurse Cancer Services

" *Anger can cover up feelings of sadness. Anger seems to be socially more acceptable than sadness. Especially men find it often easier to shake their fists rather than shed tears.* **"**
Nick Smith, Social Worker

" *To be useful you have to engage with people - which is an uncomfortable feeling because you are laying yourself open. But to be effective you have to do this ...* **"**
Frances Sheldon, Social Work Teacher

The Key Issues

Let the angry relative tell you their story first. Do not start by being defensive or jumping in with false assurances - "It wasn't like that at all" or "You'll feel better later".

Do not ask probing questions yet - let the relatives tell you how they feel. Anger needs expression - so ask gentle questions to help this process.

"You sound really upset - tell me what's happened."

What Should You Try To Find Out?

Why anger now?

- What is it about?
- Has something just happened to trigger it?
- Against whom is it directed?
- Is it legitimate?

More Facts and Comments

It is likely that different members of the family feel different emotions. Watch out for the quiet ones. Involve them too: "Do you feel/see things the same way as ...?"

66 *You can't know about the complexity of every human being - to predict and prevent anger occurring, you need to be aware that this is a partnership and you can't always know where the anger is coming from"* 99
Frances Sheldon, Social Work Teacher

Culture and gender will influence the expression of anger. While it is not possible to be specific, it is important to consider that different cultures have different ways of expressing themselves.

For example, women from many cultures would have great difficulty expressing anger towards a male doctor. A French or Italian family will typically express their grief in a more explicit and dramatic manner than a British family.

The Key Issues	More Facts and Comments

Where are we?

- Is this the right place to talk, e.g. the middle of the ward?
- Are other people listening?
- Is the patient within earshot?

How can I give this appropriate priority?

- Can I delegate part of my work?
- Am I the most appropriate person to deal with it?

What Do You Do?

Provide a safe environment. The relatives can express their anger in your presence or you can help with whoever or whatever has caused their anger.

"Let's move to ..."

"Come with me and we'll discuss this in ..."

" *Sometimes people feel uncomfortable with the label 'anger'. They will be helped to talk if you use terms like: feeling upset, expressing your views strongly, making sure people are in no doubt how you feel, being quite forceful.* "
Nick Smith, Social Worker

Beware of mood mismatches. If you appear very calm and slightly distanced, this can make an angry person even more angry.

" *Being caught up in a big system (hospital) which you feel is benevolent yet with terrible things happening. Grappling with conflicting emotions.* "
J Davies, Mother

The Key Issues

Be sympathetic.
- Give them your full attention.
- Delegate tasks where appropriate.
- Let the relatives feel you are prepared to listen to their agenda.
- Identify the key issues with the relative.

Aim to reach some agreed plan - depending on the source of the anger.
- It may be merely to talk again in more detail.
- It may be to review the patient's treatment plan.

Help the relatives to feel that
- being angry about the prospective or actual loss of a loved one is normal.
- anger can help to move things on and get things done.

More Facts and Comments

Do not look at your watch, play with your pen or nervously play with your fingers.

"I can spend 20 minutes with you now. What do you need to look at as a priority?"

You may want to involve another member of the team or refer to an agency outside the hospital.

The open expression of feelings is useful. It clears the air, allowing people to move on, to negotiate and get things done.

The Key Issues	*More Facts and Comments*
Develop a joint strategy with the relatives to cope better with the situation.	
Involve the relatives in preventing the build-up of tension.	You might say to the relatives: "What danger signals, which would tell us things are getting difficult for you, do we need to look out for?"

How Do You Know If You Have Been Effective?

Looking back

Reflect on whether you, or other members of the team, picked up cues from relatives. Did you record conversations that might have helped you better understand this situation?

- Did the relatives feel involved, have enough information?
- Did you make yourself available?
- Did the relatives pick up and convey the patient's distress?

The Key Issues

Looking forward

Remember that relatives may need extra support (e.g. Macmillan service).

Consider the potential financial worries.

Record any angry incidents in the notes and raise the significant issues with the team.

Also make contact with other relatives or patients who may have been present. You might like to involve other team members in this.

More Facts and Comments

There may be dependent children or elderly relatives.

" *You might involve the social worker in setting up a family meeting or a family/professional meeting.* "
Nick Smith, Social Worker

Remember to take care of yourself. Making yourself available to relatives and encouraging them to express their feelings openly can be exhausting.

It can often be harder to handle the reactions of other patients or other relatives who were around when relatives got angry - and who feel "Will I behave like that when it happens to me?"

" *Sometimes other patients and relatives put the shutters up - but you do need good assessment skills.* "
Frances Sheldon, Social Work Teacher

B17   *You Wonder if the Relatives are Overstressed*

The Key Issues	More Facts and Comments
What Do You Think About?	

What Do You Think About?

The duration of the patient's illness.

The relationships within the family.

The stage of the patient's illness, e.g. whether new information has been shared, new treatment begun.

The dependence of the patient on the relatives.

The other demands made on relatives.

Support given to the relatives from their own social network as well as professionals.

The physical and psychological consequences of stress.

Financial pressures as a result of illness.

66 *Sometimes when a cancer patient is readmitted to the ward, it's often the relatives whose appearance has changed the most.* 99
Ward Sister

66 *Preventive health care, for the family, is not a luxury - but ultimately much more cost effective, significantly reducing the sum of human suffering that would otherwise be needlessly shouldered.* 99
Nick Smith, Social Worker

Angry relatives - B16   Time with relatives - B19   Patient does not want the family to know how ill they are - B5

The Key Issues	*More Facts and Comments*

What Should You Try To Find Out?

Ask your team colleagues about their perception of the relatives' stress.

Explore how the family is coping with the patient at home.

Which community services are already involved?

Is the patient being supported by a social worker or clinical nurse specialist in a therapeutic relationship?

To what extent is the GP aware of the patient's current situation and needs?

District nurses, Macmillan nurses, domiciliary care (home help, meals on wheels), hospice day care, Crossroads, may all be available.

The Key Issues	More Facts and Comments

What Do You Do?

Talk with the family and try to identify areas where the health-care team can help. They may need

- more regular communication about changes in treatment
- more support at home with the patient
- financial help
- relief from long periods of visiting
- encouragement to deal with their own health problems
- more help with exploring their own feelings
- help to meet and talk as a family about their concern.

Do call in additional support where appropriate, e.g. social workers.

Try to provide more support in a co-ordinated way as a team.

" *If we are aware of the problem-solving urge in most families, we can help them change successfully rather than making them dependent on us.* "
Nick Smith, Social Worker

The Key Issues	More Facts and Comments

Do plan for continuing support when the patient is to be discharged, e.g. local Macmillan service. It would be useful to explore this with the patient's GP.

How Do You Know If You Have Been Effective?

Looking back

It may be worthwhile reviewing if stress in relatives is something that is assessed regularly as part of your care.

Looking forward

You may well see a considerable difference in a family which has been able to discuss its problems. The key issue is to tap into existing coping strategies and help develop them.

B18   *The Relatives are Crying*

The Key Issues	*More Facts and Comments*
What Do You Think About?	
The current status of the patient.	Changes in treatment, or changes in the appearance of the patient, may bring the relatives closer to an awareness of loss.
	The family unit is more than a group of people related to one another. Family members communicate, share emotions and have a dependence on one another. I Lichter (1987)
The level of **stress in the family**.	Exhausted families may be more ready to release their feelings.
The relationships between the patient and the family.	In close relationships, distress is usually related to loss, while in more distant relationships distress may be associated with guilt feelings.
The hospital environment.	If the patient was recently admitted to hospital, the relatives may feel relief. They may also feel guilty about not continuing to care for the patient at home.
The relationship *you* have with the family.	The quality of your relationship with the family will help you understand and be able to talk with them.

The Key Issues

What Should You Try To Find Out?

Has something happened recently?

Do they prefer to be alone or do they need some privacy and direct support from someone in the team?

Is someone else already helping?

What Do You Do?

Find some privacy for them.

Provide them with an opportunity to talk.

Provide them with space in which they can express their feelings.

As with other strong feelings, ensure the family know that crying is fully accepted.

More Facts and Comments

Sometimes things can get routine for us - you have to remember how unique this situation is for the family.

This can be difficult to assess but may require a gentle question: "What would help now?" or "Would you like me to stay for a while?"

There can be nothing worse than several members of the team all trying to help in different ways at the same time.

The Key Issues	*More Facts and Comments*
It can be appropriate, for some people, to comfort them through touch.	Enquire first: "How do you comfort each other ... with physical contact or with words?"

It can be appropriate, for some people, to comfort them through touch.

Review the level of support and information this family is already receiving from the team. Discuss how this could be improved.

If appropriate, discuss with the family or refer to other colleagues, e.g. social worker.

Make sure that other members of the team are aware of the relatives' distress and are able to continue to support this family.

How Do You Know If You Have Been Effective?

Ask the family if support could have been more useful if provided differently.

Enquire first: "How do you comfort each other ... with physical contact or with words?"

The Key Issues

Looking back

It can be of value to reflect on your own level of comfort or discomfort when the relatives were crying.

Do you think you could have responded more appropriately? Ask colleagues how they feel.

Looking forward

Family support will remain part of your remit. You may like to consider the openness of communication in the family - and whether the patient is aware of the relatives' distress.

More Facts and Comments

B19   *You Do Not have Enough Time to Talk with Relatives*

The Key Issues	More Facts and Comments

What Do You Think About?

Is time shortage a reality or a defence?

Does it need to be you? Perhaps someone else might be able to talk with them, e.g. the charge nurse.

Are you needing to *impart new information* or is it part of your regular relationship with the family?

What Should You Try To Find Out?

How long are the relatives available in the ward?

Is someone else available to talk with them?

Is it possible to delegate some of your other work?

Professionals can sometimes find themselves making excuses, when they are dealing with distressing situations.

Regular meetings with the family may pre-empt, or reduce, anxiety.

The Key Issues	More Facts and Comments

What Do You Do?

If no time is available now, and no one else can either talk with relatives, or take over some of your other work, suggest a time when you *will* be available.

Try to organise yourself to have time available to talk with relatives.

Aim to help relatives feel confident.   Engage them in managing your joint time.

Visit the patient during visiting time.   Use that as an opportunity to talk with the family.

Agree a pattern of 'availability' with other members of the team, e.g. charge nurse, senior house officer, staff nurse.

Always write up conversations in the case-notes.   Make these available to other members of the team.

For example, you could suggest: I've got ten minutes now, because I need to go to the clinic, but I could speak to you at 3 pm tomorrow for longer."

66*When it comes to giving time the answer can often be 'little and often'. You need to be practical and decide when and how often you can meet.* 99
Nick Smith, Social Worker

The Key Issues	*More Facts and Comments*

How Do You Know If You Have Been Effective?

Looking back

You may never be able to assess this completely. Reviewing your time planning may improve matters.

Looking forward

In the midst of all the pressures on your time, continue to plan to meet the needs of relatives. You could raise this issue at one of the multiprofessional meetings.

The Key Issues	*More Facts and Comments*

What Do You Think About?

What does the family already know about the disease?

What are their expectations of the results of treatment?

What recent events have occurred that indicate treatment is not effective?

Uncertainty, for the patient and relatives, can be one of the most distressing experiences.

What Should You Try To Find Out?

What changes have occurred in the physical state of the patient?

Are the patient's symptoms well controlled?

What is the patient's perception of the effectiveness of treatment?

Can you meet patient and relatives together?

> *It can be easy to talk with the patient who is ready to talk about dying ... but what about the relatives, they will need us more at this point ... but that's much more difficult.*
> Kate Copp, Macmillan Nurse Teacher

Explain to patient treatment not working - B2

The Key Issues

What Do You Do?

Provide time and privacy to talk *with* the relatives, asking for their perception of the situation.

Do not react against any anger that may be expressed. Be prepared to listen. Some criticisms may be valid.

Make sure patient and relatives are not left with different sets of information.

How Do You Know If You Have Been Effective?

Looking back

It takes courage for relatives to ask difficult questions like this - but they approached *you*, which may well be an indicator of the rapport you have developed.

Looking forward

Keep up an open dialogue with the patient and family. Look around to see if there are other relatives who need to talk to you about the patient, but may not have had the opportunity.

More Facts and Comments

"*It's useful to discuss with relatives how they will share or can be helped to share new information with the patient.*"
Nick Smith, Social Worker

The Key Issues	More Facts and Comments

What Do You Think About?

The relatives can be an important resource in assessing the patient's experience of pain. If they feel the patient is in pain now, this requires an immediate response.

What Should You Try To Find Out?

How is the patient's pain being assessed?

What is the management of the pain?

"Sometimes unresolved emotional or spiritual pain exacerbates physical pain or makes it seem unbearable. "
Nick Smith, Social Worker

What Do You Do?

Review the patient's treatment. Ensure it is appropriate and adequate for the patient's pain.

If the patient is in pain, respond immediately.

Explore with relatives their perception of the patient's experience and any other anxieties they may have.

The relatives' anxiety may be influencing their perception of the patient's pain.

Where the pain problem is particularly difficult, refer to a pain clinic or hospice.

The Key Issues	*More Facts and Comments*

How Do You Know If You Have Been Effective?

Looking back

Two issues for reflection:

- Has pain assessment and management been appropriate?
- Has communication with the relatives been consistent?

Looking forward

Review the relatives' complaint of too much pain. Review pain assessment and treatment strategies used.

B22   *Relatives Ask You Why the Patient is Not Being Fed*

The Key Issues	*More Facts and Comments*
What Do You Think About?	
Anorexia and cachexia are associated with cancer.	Tumours, particularly in liver stomach or pancreas, can cause a feeling of 'fullness'. Decreased interest in food can be associated with external compression or partial restriction of the gastro-intestinal tract. Food aversion can occur (protein, beef or pork). *Nutrition is often a major issue and concern of terminally ill patients and their families.* *C R Gallagher-Alfred (1991)*
The meaning of 'food' and nutrition in advanced cancer.	*Food carries biological, emotional and sociological meanings. It means different things to different people depending on whether they are ill or well.* *C R Gallagher-Alfred (1991)*
Physical changes, associated with disease, influence desire for food, e.g. • alterations in gastric absorption and an increase in nutrient requirements • reduced rates of gastric emptying.	Medical interventions, e.g. chemotherapy, may increase nutrient requirements. Narcotics alter nutrition needs - side-effects of nausea, vomiting or constipation occur.
Psychological changes - depressed patients are often anorectic and do not eat.	

The Key Issues	*More Facts and Comments*

What Should You Try To Find Out?

What is the family's perception of the health status of the patient and the nutritional support needed?

Does the family feel that, if the patient doesn't eat, he or she will die sooner?

Is the family concerned that lack of food or fluid will increase suffering?

Dehydration has been called a natural anaesthesia for terminally ill patients because it appears to decrease the patient's perception of suffering by reducing the level of consciousness.
C R Gallagher-Alfred (1991)

Does the family believe in the more unorthodox nutritional therapies?

These include: the Bristol Cancer Diet (vegetarian/organic), high doses of vitamin C.

Are there underlying emotional problems within the family?

Sometimes, if patients are not eating, the family can defuse their own guilt towards their loved one by projecting on to the patient or the staff that the patient is not trying.

The Key Issues	*More Facts and Comments*

The patient's perspective

Is the patient nauseated or vomiting?

Does the patient have a sore or dry mouth?

Is there difficulty swallowing or chewing?

Is he or she in pain, depressed?

Does the patient have diarrhoea or constipation?

Does he or she take vitamin supplements?

What does the weight loss and poor appetite mean to the patient?

The team plan

With the dietitian closely involved, review decisions about how aggressive the plan will be to correct the problem of **anorexia**.

If anorexia is due to correctable causes and the patient has a predicted life expectancy of several months, the correctable causes should be treated aggressively if desired by the patient.
C R Gallagher-Alfred (1991)

The Key Issues	*More Facts and Comments*

What Do You Do?

Your response to the family will reflect the decisions jointly made with the patient, the family and the team about nutritional support.

Do listen to the family carefully.

Do explain how anorexia, body image and body function all relate.

Do help the family to reduce their 'pressure' on the patient to eat.

It can be more appropriate to offer the patient no food unless requested.

Use phrases like
- "Let him eat whenever and whatever he likes."
- "If you push her to eat she'll feel uncomfortable."
- "Don't worry that he is not eating - it doesn't seem to worry him."

The family may be helped if you give them an active role.

Do ensure well-fitting clothes and avoid full-length mirrors in bathrooms.

Do review your assessment of the patient.

The Key Issues	*More Facts and Comments*

How Do You Know If You Have Been Effective?

Looking back

This question from the relatives may indicate a need to be more closely involved in decision making. However, they have had the confidence to ask you.

Looking forward

You will need to understand that the change in eating patterns and appearance will be difficult for the family, who will continue to need your support.

B23 The Relative Asks if He or She Can Sleep with the Patient

The Key Issues	More Facts and Comments

What Do You Think About?

There are very practical reasons for intimacy or sexual contact. Intimate sexual contact is a normal part of relationships. Physical closeness, if not necessarily sexual intercourse, is for many couples especially important in times of illness. Institutions like hospitals do not generally facilitate intimate contact between patient and partner. Such closeness

- can suppress pain
- allows a feeling of normality, of being valued
- increases self-esteem and emotional equilibrium
- communicates security, warmth and caring.

Sexuality is an integral part of every human being ... it is more than a physical expression, it is about self concept, self esteem and social role, which combine to form the identity of the person.
S Poorman (1983)

" *Sometimes it's the members of staff that have the problems: "This is a patient, this is a hospital - we can't have that."* "
Gill Oliver, Regional Nurse Cancer Services

" *There are also taboos about the propriety of sexual needs of patients which influence our response to such a request.* "
Nick Smith, Social Worker

The Key Issues	*More Facts and Comments*

Physical difficulties in sexual activity may be due to
- pain and fatigue
- nausea, vomiting, bowel disturbances, discharging wounds
- radiotherapy, cytotoxic chemotherapy
- lack of sexual response, caused by swelling involving genitalia, by vascular impairment or by nerve damage.

What Should You Try To Find Out?

The fact that you were the one who was asked, suggests you are seen as approachable. It does take courage to ask this question in hospital.

What does the patient want?

Sexual health problems presented by patients and partners sometimes go unheard.
M Rutherford and D Foxley (1991)

Patients with sex-specific cancer, breast or prostate, are more likely than other patients to experience sexual adjustment problems.
B J Hailey and K N Hardin (1988)

Some patients have neither the ability nor the urge for full sexual intercourse, yet intimacy and human contact are desired.
L Leiber et al (1976)

The Key Issues	*More Facts and Comments*

What are your own, and the team's views on the patient's sexuality and its expression?

What is the organisational response or policy?

Are you in a position to decide?

What Do You Do?

If the organisation agrees, then together with the team, you should

- arrange accommodation
- organise privacy
- check with the patient and partner whether they need to discuss possible difficulties.

Bear in mind that couples may not ask explicitly. You should enquire: "Do you manage to find time and space to be close to one another?" or "How does the illness affect your life as partners?"

The Key Issues	*More Facts and Comments*

If the organisation does not agree

- do not feel disempowered
- generate a discussion to help the organisation to change
- look at the potential for the patient to have time at home.

How Do You Know If You Have Been Effective?

Looking back

Could you have anticipated this need sooner?

Looking forward

Now that this issue has been raised for a specific patient, would it be useful to consider its importance for other patients and families?

B24 A Staff Member Asks You: "Why don't we let this patient die in peace?"

The Key Issues	More Facts and Comments

What Do You Think About?

You may initially feel defensive but you are obviously perceived as approachable. This question may indicate

- a different perception of the problem
- a lack of awareness of the rationale for current management
- new information about which you are not aware
- a stressed member of staff, overidentifying with the patient.

What Should You Try To Find Out?

What are this staff member's perceptions of management and what is their relationship with the patient?

Thou shalt not kill; but needst not strive officiously to keep alive.
A H Clough (1819-1861)

" *The student nurse asked me why a nasogastric tube was needed so near her death - but without it, the lack of control over her obstruction would have been impossible and very distressing for her husband.* "
Gill Oliver, Regional Nurse Cancer Services

Particular individuals can be identified by the patient with whom they will discuss their real fears. These 'cues' may not be available to all of the team.

" *It can be useful to use another staff member's concern as a source of information - that perhaps this patient's pain (existential, spiritual or emotional) is not being adequately addressed.* "
Nick Smith, Social Worker

The Key Issues	More Facts and Comments

Has something happened recently to act as a trigger to change the management, e.g. patient's pain changed, patient talking about death more explicity, relatives distressed?

In a busy ward where the patient may be surrounded by hustle and bustle, or they see others getting on well but their own life slipping away.
I Lichter (1987)

What Do You Do?

Be prepared to listen to the other person's point of view. If this is the worst time for a discussion because you are dealing with a crisis elsewhere - plan to meet as soon as possible over coffee/lunch.

Discuss the rationale for current treatment to ensure the staff member understands.

Share any relevant conversations that either of you have had with the patient. Has he or she expressed a concern about too much interventionist care being given.

A person's views on when to treat or not to treat must be influenced by their upbringing, spiritual attitude, professional background and private conscience.

Those that have cared for the very sick know that it is possible to maintain a policy of continual and sometimes aggressive intervention, without conviction that it will help, sometimes at extreme psychological and physical distress to the patient and relatives.
T Hunt (1991)

The Key Issues

Talk with the patient to explore the issues raised.

Reassess the level of pain, symptom control or anxiety about health status.

Relay new information to the team and your senior, so that the management plan can be reviewed, if appropriate.

How Do You Know If You Have Been Effective?

The original question suggests that one staff member believes this patient is not dying in peace. To be effective, you will have made enquiries and reviewed management to check this perception.

More Facts and Comments

In an ideal world it could be argued that care of the living should be so good that euthanasia is unwarranted. The problem remains how can the law protect everyone and yet recognise the individual's right to foreshorten a suffering life? After all, this is a principle of patient autonomy. But can this be reconciled with professional ethics and social conscience?
T Hunt (1991)

The Key Issues	*More Facts and Comments*

You will have been effective

- if you *have not* dismissed this question
- if you *have reviewed* the management plan
- even if the treatment remains the same.

Looking back

It may be useful to review the communication network within the team. Perhaps these issues need to be discussed more openly, more frequently.

Looking forward

Both for this patient, and others, regular discussion about quality of life needs to occur. Your openness and readiness for debate will facilitate this.

❝*I would be interested to know if the patient had an opportunity to consider elements of the quality of life, and to specify at what point treatment should stop.*❞
Nick Smith, Social Worker

B25   *A Patient Dies - What Do You Say to Relatives?*

There is no single *right* way to respond to relatives when the patient has died. Probably, you will already have developed a relationship with both the patient and the family. You may well be feeling sad yourself. Your professionalism and humanity will be needed at this point. You must find the words and manner that best suit you.

What Do You Think About?

The nature of the death.

- Were you present at the death?
- Were the relatives present?

The relationships between the patient and the family.

The privacy needed by this family now.

> 66 *Doctors are in a good position to help relatives to begin to grieve following the death. Relatives will remember your approach at this time vividly. You cannot make this 'good' or 'not hurt'. Grief is painful.* 99
> Kate Copp, Macmillan Nurse Teacher

The Key Issues	More Facts and Comments

Do other people need to be there - e.g. other family or team members who had a close relationship with the patient?

Do you need to reorganise, reprioritise your patient care?

What Should You Try To Find Out?

What are the relatives feeling?

What may the family wish to say to you?

What do they want to do *now* e.g.

- see the patient again?
- take the patient's belongings now?
- go home?
- contact other relatives who may come to the hospital for support or come to take them home?

"*Rather than inviting a report of how they are feeling, enable the family to realise that any expressions they may wish to make are normal and useful.***"**
Nick Smith, Social Worker

They may wish to see their relative after death - either alone or with you.

Communication Around Death

The Key Issues

What Do You Do?
Express your own feelings, simply: "I am very sorry".

Confirm that death has occurred - use the words "is dead" or "has died".

Give clear but caring messages.

Give the relatives opportunity and time to ask you questions - to aid their understanding of the situation.

Offer practical help from yourself or the hospital.

How Do You Know If You Have Been Effective?
Contact the patient's GP. If relevant, comment on how the relatives are currently responding to their loss.

More Facts and Comments

Talk about what made this patient special and how he or she will be remembered by the staff.

❝ *It is useful to focus on the positive aspects: patient died peacefully, with relatives there, without pain.* ❞
Nick Smith, Social Worker

❝ *You can't make the person feel better and they can't help you by appearing helped.* ❞
Colin Murray-Parkes, Psychiatrist

The Key Issues

More Facts and Comments

Check out your approach with a colleague. (You may wish to see the family with one of the nursing staff - you will then be able to provide feedback to one another, afterwards.)

Looking back

Inevitably, the patient's death will cause you to reflect on your own performance as well as that of the team. Perhaps you could look at the relationship with the relatives and whether it could have been improved.

You may want to talk with colleagues about how this patient and their family were managed. Were there any lessons to be learned?

Looking forward

What support is available now for this family?

Discuss with the family what difficulties they anticipate, how they think they will handle them and whether they would like professional help.

Be aware of previous 'danger signals' which indicate that relatives might find it difficult to cope with the loss:

- denial by patient/relatives of the seriousness of the illness
- fights/disagreements between patient and family
- pressure for treatment at all costs
- recent bereavement.

"*Think about offering support/referring to the social worker at an early stage.* Nick Smith, Social Worker **"**

The Key Issues	More Facts and Comments

What Do You Think About?

There are practical issues to consider when a patient dies. Information on these will help the relatives:

- collecting the death certificate
- post-mortem requests
- undertakers
- procedure for cremation or burial
- bereavement follow up.

Also, remember that this may be the first time some relatives or carers have seen a dead body.

You may consider attending the funeral yourself if the relatives specifically invite you to do so.

" *Distress will affect how much the relatives can remember. I usually say there are three things they need to do.*

1   *Contact other family/friends.*
2   *Take the medical certificate to the Registrar.*
3   *Phone an undertaker who will remember all the big things as well as all the small things they will need to do.* **"**

J M Leiper, Consultant in Palliative Medicine

The Key Issues	*More Facts and Comments*

What Should You Try To Find Out?

Were these relatives present at the death of the patient?

Was the death distressing?

What are the cultural and religious roles in this family?

Who is the key person to organise issues?

If the relative is alone, can anyone else come to be with them, travel home with them.

Is a post-mortem request necessary?

Do the relatives wish to see the patient after death?

The Key Issues	**More Facts and Comments**

What Do You Do?

Answer any questions they may have. Offer the use of a telephone and private room to contact other family members.

A useful resource for the relative is D Nuttal, 'The Early Days of Grieving', Beaconsfield, Beaconsfield Publishers, 1991.

If they are willing, encourage them to view the body, talk to the deceased, touch the body and begin to say goodbye.

Contact the chaplain or other religious adviser, if appropriate.

The Registrar can provide additional copies of the certificate for life insurance purposes or to claim social security money. Most people find it helpful to obtain two or three copies at the time.
D Nuttal (1991)

Discuss how the medical certificate can be obtained and the death registered.

Ask if they have made contact with an undertaker and how they can view their relative again, if they wish, in the chapel of rest.

This can be useful for relatives who were not be present when the patent died.

Explain, if asked, how cremation can be arranged.

"*I usually say that I will contact both the GP as well as other doctors who have been involved in the care. This prevents the family getting clinic appointment cards at a later date. It is essential to contact the GP.*"
J M Leiper, Consultant in Palliative Medicine

Offer advice about help in the future, including bereavement support.

The Key Issues	*More Facts and Comments*

How Do You Know If You Have Been Effective?

Looking back

Reflect with your colleagues on how well this family were prepared for this death and on how well they are coping.

Could any more have been done, e.g. more time spent with the family?

Looking forward

Have you another family about to be in a similar situation? Can you and the team help them to prepare for their loss?

How are you looking after yourself?

Useful Resources

Leaflet D49 - *'What to do after a death'*. Department of Social Security, DSS Leaflets Unit, PO Box 21, Stanmore, Middlesex   HA71AY.

Leaflet FB 29 - *'Help when someone dies'*. A guide to social security benefits. DSS Leaflets Unit, PO Box 21, Stanmore, Middlesex HA7 1AY.

B27   *A Patient Has Died - What Do You Say to Other Patients?*

The Key Issues	More Facts and Comments

What Do You Think About?

You may well think that most patients in the ward have enough problems without talking about someone who has just died. However, patients are usually aware that a death has occurred in the ward. They often do not need to be told.

For the patients, this may be their closest contact with death. Staff may see death as more routine.

For a patient with a similar condition, identification may be occurring: "He had what I've got - does that mean I'm going to die?"

A patient dying in the ward can have adverse effects on other patients.

Much unhappiness has come into the world because of new bewilderment and things left unsaid.
F Dostoevsky (1821-1881)

We talk about sex but not about death.
Kate Copp, Macmillan Nurse Teacher

We must believe that people who are also patients can cope with honesty expressed in a caring way.
Frances Sheldon, Social Work Teacher

Uncertainty seems to be the hardest experience of all for the psyche to bear.

If a person does not know what action can be taken, he or she can do nothing, just remain helplessly paralysed or distressed and agitated.

This can be true. It is often the reason why 'dying patients' are moved into single rooms as a precursor to death. However, anxiety may be increased by this process, for the patient, the family and those who remain in the ward.

The Key Issues	More Facts and Comments

What Should You Try To Find Out?

If you were not present, find out about the nature of the death, i.e. the factors that might influence the other patients.

Was the death peaceful?

What was the relationship between other patients and the one who has died?

What Do You Do?

Be honest.

You may not have to tell but to find out what each patient knows and may wish to talk about.

The Key Issues

Heed non-verbal and verbal cues from patients.

Ask other members of the team to be involved. Ask yourself if you are the most appropriate person to speak to other patients.

Allow patients to ask questions, to help dispel misconceptions about what took place. "I wondered if you wanted to ask me any questions?"

Use phrases like "has died" rather than euphemisms such as "was taken from us".

Do not be afraid to show the human side of yourself.

Do protect the confidentiality of the patient who has died.

More Facts and Comments

Patients are also very receptive to the non-verbal cues of medical practitioners. Non-verbal cues are generally decoded with a fair degree of accuracy, but accuracy may be lost when either party is frightened.

The Key Issues	*More Facts and Comments*

How Do You Know If You Have Been Effective?

This may not be easy to assess. Look for indicators, e.g. the ease with which these patients subsequently talk to you and the relationship you have with them.

Ask colleagues for constructive feedback about the way you handled the situation.

Looking back

Were you aware of how other patients and perhaps their relatives, were feeling before the patient died?

Looking forward

Try to use what patients say to you to influence how you will assess patient needs in a similar situation.

Monitor these patients for continued distress. Ensure the team is aware of what happened.

B28   *A Patient Has a Distressing Death - What Do You Say to Other Patients?*

The Key Issues	*More Facts and Comments*

What Do You Think About?

Think about how the patient died.

- Was he or she vomiting excessively?
- Were they disfigured?
- Was he or she dyspnoeic?
- Were they moaning?
- Were relatives present or was the patient alone?

Think about the effect on other adjacent patients.

- Do they have a similar disease and identify with the patient?
- What relationship did they have with that patient and family?

Other patients in the vicinity of a patient who has had a distressing death may not be talking about it. This does not mean that they have not noticed what has happened.

❝*Sometimes - when the death has been distressing with symptoms difficult to control - there can be a great relief it is all over. But there is also fear that it might happen to them.*❞
Sue Skidmore, Macmillan Tutor

The Key Issues	*More Facts and Comments*
Think about the effect this patient's death is having on you.	Medical staff can feel impotent when symptoms prove impossible to control completely. The feeling of having 'failed' the patient can extend to the whole of the team.

What Should You Try To Find Out?

Someone else in the team may already have discussed this with other patients.

Find out what the team response to this situation is going to be - you may not be the only person talking to these patients.

What is appropriate to say to patients, to avoid breaching confidentiality?

Are there any behavioural changes that might suggest anxiety in other patients, e.g. insomnia, appetite reduced.

The Key Issues	*More Facts and Comments*

What Do You Do?

Try to find out how the other patients feel and give them time to express their feelings.

"It is sad about Mrs Dawes ..." or "We are sorry about what has happened ..."

Make open statements to allow the patient room for expression.

Somehow, transmit to patients that this type of death is not the norm, e.g: "The way that this disease affected that patient was unusual."

Provide an opportunity for the patient to talk to you about this at another time, if appropriate.

Review any physical changes in other patients and manage accordingly, e.g. a patient may have difficulty in sleeping.

Turning a blind eye may seem a way of sparing the patient - but ignoring the obvious is likely to set up a barrier between patient and doctor.

The Key Issues	More Facts and Comments

How Do You Know If You Have Been Effective?

The fact that you and the team are addressing the issue may help patients to discuss any concerns or problems they have. This will ultimately reduce anxiety.

Looking back

Reflect on whether it would have been useful to help patients prepare for this situation or to provide more privacy for them.

Looking forward

These patients will still need supporting.

Keep other members of the team updated on relevant conversations. (Write in case-notes.)

Use other members of the team for support and constructive feedback on your approach.

Section C - Distressing Symptoms

Section C: Distressing Symptoms - An Overview

- Dyspnoea

- Dysphagia
- Nausea
- Vomiting
- Constipation
- Diarrhoea

- Dry/sore mouth
- Halitosis
- Anorexia

- Sleeping problems
- Fatigue
- Restlessness
- Twitching

- Lymphoedema
- Skin lesions
- Sweating

C1   *The Patient Has Halitosis*

The Key Issues	*More Facts and Comments*

What Do You Think About?

Is it a problem for

- the patient?
- those caring for the patient?

Halitosis is foul or unpleasant-smelling breath.

Patients are often not aware of halitosis and it goes without saying that it is a source of great distress and embarrassment to relatives.
D Doyle and T F Benton (1991)

What Should You Try To Find Out?

- Is it due to the patient's diet? Does the patient have a diet of heavily flavoured or spicy foods?
- Is there evidence of a local cause in the patient's mouth, e.g. infected teeth, gums, oral mucosa, or oral carcinoma?
- Is there an obvious cause in the upper gastro-intestinal tract, such as reflux associated with gastric stasis or gastric carcinoma, particularly linitis plastica (cesspool halitosis)?
- Does the patient have an anaerobic infection of the chest, e.g. bronchiectasis?

Diet is a frequent cause, especially the use of garlic or spices.

The commonest mouth infection is candidiasis, but this alone is unlikely to cause halitosis. Anaerobic infection of the gums often causes halitosis. It is easily treated with oral metronidazole (400 mg twice daily).

Reflux of stomach contents into the oesophagus may cause halitosis. This can be treated with drugs such as metoclopramide (10 mg four times daily), domperidone (10-20 mg four times daily) or cisapride (10 mg three times daily before meals).

Anaerobic infection of the lungs can cause particularly troublesome halitosis. Again, it may be treated with systemic metronidazole.

The Key Issues	*More Facts and Comments*

What Do You Do?

- Treat any obvious infection. The choice of drug depends on results of culture and on the patient's sensitivity.
- Pay careful attention to **oral and dental hygiene.**
- Suggest the use of flavoured mints or other similar products.

Energetic attention to oral hygiene is essential in all cancer patients. Dentures must be cleaned regularly - preferably in 0.2% chlorhexidine gluconate. It is also important to ensure adequate fluid intake.

If the mouth is excessively dry as a result of disease or irradiation, artificial salivas could help.

"*If no obvious cause of halitosis is found it is reasonable to treat the patient empirically with a five day course of metronidazole, 200 mg three times daily by mouth.***"***
W M O'Neill, Consultant in Palliative Medicine

How Do You Know If You Have Been Effective?

- Review the problem with the patient and, if appropriate, the carers.
- Treat the halitosis if it recurs.

The Key Issues

What Do You Think About?

It is normal for reduced activity to decrease energy intake. It is also natural for people who are seriously ill to lose interest in food. However, it is essential in anorexia, which causes great anxiety for the carers, to consider the causes.

Is it a natural disinterest (primary anorexia), or due to some reversible cause (secondary anorexia)?

What Should You Try to Find Out?

Establish if the patient has any reversible cause, or is on any drugs that may diminish appetite.

More Facts and Comments

Primary anorexia is common in patients with advanced malignancy.

Secondary anorexia could be due to candidiasis and other causes of **sore and painful mouth, nausea** with or without fear of **vomiting** after food, pain, constipation, early satiation, fatigue, unappetising food, odours in environment, depression, metabolic causes such as **hypercalcaemia** and uraemia.

Occasionally drugs may be implicated, such as antibiotics or drugs that can cause nausea.

Concomitant radiotherapy or chemotherapy may cause anorexia.

The Key Issues	More Facts and Comments

What Do You Do?

Treat any underlying cause and, if a particular drug appears to be the cause, modify drug regimen.

Advise on appropriate dietary measures, taking account of the flavours, consistency and quantity of food.

Dietary tips

The patient may be tempted by minute helpings on the smallest plate available.

Attractively served food, at frequent intervals unrelated to standard meal times, is more likely to be eaten.

A small alcoholic drink of the patient's choice, as an aperitif, may help.

Food should be available when the patient is hungry. A microwave oven helps to achieve this.

Be reluctant to offer 'invalid' food no matter how nutritious, but ever ready to permit and encourage any bizarre fancy the patient may have even if it is a 'Chinese carry-out', kippers during the night, lager at breakfast, stout with added sugar.
D Doyle and T F Benton (1991)

The Key Issues	**More Facts and Comments**

Consider the use of corticosteroids as appetite stimulants for patients in whom no identifiable cause can be found:

- prednisolone 15-30 mg daily, or
- dexamethasone 2-4 mg daily.

More recently, medroxyprogesterone acetate, 100 mg three times daily, has also been shown to act as an appetite stimulant. It may offer an advantage over dexamethasone, because it appears to have fewer side-effects.

How Do You Know If You Have Been Effective?

Review the patient frequently. Offer clear explanations and reassurance to both the patient and family.

Looking forward

Anorexia often causes greater anxiety for the **family** than for the patient. It is important to listen and to understand the family's fears. Be prepared to offer basic psychological support in response to their worries.

Emphasise that you are not too concerned whether the patient gets a rounded diet.

"*He must eat or he will die.*"
A wife

"*Just give him a little of what he fancies.*"
A doctor

"*I shall be happy even if he just takes fluids.*"
A doctor

"*After all, babies thrive on milk.*"
A doctor

C3 *The Patient Has a Sore Mouth*

The Key Issues	*More Facts and Comments*

Anything which makes eating or swallowing difficult is worth considering promptly, for the sake of the patient and the relatives. The patient's suffering will be increased by such difficulties. The relative's anxiety will be greater, too, if they feel deprived of feeding the patient - all that was left to them.

What Do You Think About?

Common causes of sore mouth are

- oral infection and ulceration

  Oral infections are common in advanced disease, more so when oral hygiene has been neglected. Candidiasis is the most common cause of oral infection and is usually obvious as a raw oral mucosa coated with white plaques. Aphthous ulcers are much less common than oral candidiasis.

- malnutrition (hypovitaminosis, anaemia, protein deficiency)
- drugs
  - cytotoxic drugs may cause marked stomatitis
  - antibiotics

The Key Issues	More Facts and Comments

- **dry mouth**
- oral cancer
- ill-fitting dentures.

What Should You Try To Find Out?

What does the patient complain of?

Has the patient noticed any alteration in taste?

What does examination reveal?

Patients with advanced disease tend to lose weight. Their gums may therefore shrink. Previously well-fitting dentures no longer fit adequately. Dentures can be adjusted to fit more comfortably. If necessary, a new denture can be made.

" *Food does not taste right.* "
A patient

" *Everything is tasteless.* "
A patient

" *I have a metallic taste in my mouth* "
A patient

The Key Issues	More Facts and Comments

What Do You Do?

Treat any infection or ulceration.

Candidiasis: topical nystatin suspension 2 ml four times a day, or nystatin pastilles four times daily for 7-14 days.

Resistant candidiasis: usually responds to systemic oral fluconazole (50 mg capsule daily) for 7-14 days. It may also respond to miconazole gel (5-10 ml four times daily held in the mouth).

Aphthous ulcers: hydrocortisone pellets (2.5 mg four times daily), corticosteroids in lozenges or in paste, followed by carmellose gelatin paste.

Explain to the patient with post-chemotherapy stomatitis that, given time, it will clear spontaneously. Reassure the patient that, meantime, you will be prescribing some medicine to help.

Post-chemotherapy stomatitis may be helped with Aschurt's solution (a betamethasone solution)10 ml four-hourly. This must be prepared freshly for each patient by the pharmacist.

Change drug regimens when necessary.

Explore how the patient prefers his or her food, regarding

- temperature and
- form.

The Key Issues

Ensure the maintenance of proper oral hygiene.

Arrange for the adjustment of any ill-fitting dentures.

How Do You Know If You Have Been Effective?

Review physical signs following treatment of any underlying cause.

Discuss with a dentist the feasibility of adjusting of a denture and, if necessary, the making of a new set of dentures.

The circumstances must be explained carefully to the dentist. Indicate the patient's limited prognosis, but emphasise the benefit of having a well-fitting denture for their remaining life.

More Facts and Comments

C4   *The Patient Complains of a Dry Mouth*

The Key Issues	*More Facts and Comments*

What Do You Think About?

It is important to realise that this distressing symptom can be due to many causes

- inadequate fluid intake and dehydration,
- **oral infection,**
- drugs,

- **hypercalcaemia,**
- diminution of salivary secretion as a result of previous radiotherapy to head and neck
- concurrent disease, e.g. uncontrolled diabetes,
- mouth breathing when asleep, due to debility.

Oral candida is common in patients with advanced disease. Patients frequently complain of a dry mouth.

Almost all patients on regular opioids complain of a dry mouth. Some of these patients develop tolerance to this symptom. For other patients the symptom persists.

Other drugs that may cause or contribute to a dry mouth include anticholinergic drugs, antihistamines, tricyclic **antidepressants** and diuretics.

The Key Issues	*More Facts and Comments*

What Should You Try To Find Out?

- Is the patient receiving a sufficient amount of fluid?
- Is the patient otherwise clinically hydrated?
- Is there any evidence of oral infection?
- What drugs is the patient taking?

What Do You Do?

- Ensure an adequate fluid intake.
- Give advice about oral hygiene.
- Encourage patients to suck ice cubes or frozen fruit segments, e.g. pineapple or orange.

Pineapple chunks contain a proteolytic enzyme, ananase, that also cleans the mouth. The tinned variety is better tolerated than fresh. There is no evidence that the sugar content of pineapple predisposes to candida.

- Treat any oral mucosal infection.
- Review the need to continue any causative drugs such as cyclizine, hyoscine and diuretics.
- Consider the use of artificial salivas, particularly when the dry mouth is due to compromised salivary function.

Candidiasis can be treated with nystatin (2 ml, four times daily for 7-14 days). In resistant cases, miconazole gel (5-10 ml, four times daily) can be substituted.

The Key Issues	More Facts and Comments

- Explain the situation and management to the patient and relatives.

How Do You Know If You Have Been Effective?
Review the patient daily.

Looking forward
Adequate explanation to the patient of the cause of their dry mouth frequently relieves anxiety. They then feel able to use simple measures to combat it.

C5 *The Patient Has Dysphagia*

The Key Issues	*More Facts and Comments*

What Do You Think About?

Consider whether the patient's complaint is due to true dysphagia or odynophagia. If it is true dysphagia, is it caused by a neurological deficit or by obstruction?

Odynophagia is pain on swallowing. It can be caused by conditions that lead to a **sore** or **dry mouth**, which may also result in an inflamed and painful oesophagus.

True dysphagia, inability to swallow, may be due to an intrinsic obstructive cause (e.g. tumour) in the pharynx, larynx or oesophagus. It may also be caused by extrinsic compression of the oesophagus, from a mediastinal tumour or enlarged glands. Previous high-dose radiation - aimed at curative treatment of a laryngeal, oesophageal or mediastinal tumour - may result in fibrosis and some degree of dysphagia. True dysphagia may also be due to motor neurone disease.

What Should You Try To Find Out?

Is the difficulty due to discomfort alone?

Does the patient have difficulty with both liquids and solids?

Dysphagia due to a neurological deficit is likely to present with difficulty in swallowing both liquids and solids.

Dysphagia due to an obstructive lesion will initially cause difficulty with solids alone.

The Key Issues	**More Facts and Comments**

What Do You Do?

Treat any cause of odynophagia, such as sore mouth or dry mouth.

Give advice about dietary measures, soft or liquid diet as appropriate and seek the help of a dietitian.

Consider the possible benefit of surgery, radiotherapy, chemotherapy, stenting or laser therapy for obstructive lesions, and refer as appropriate.

Consider the use of a gastrostomy or other feeding tube.

Initial treatment is attention to diet, with simple advice on the use of soft or liquid diets. In the case of possible mechanical obstruction, a trial of steroids is worthwhile. Consideration should always be given to palliative resection of a mechanical obstruction. Radiotherapy would be helpful in tumours that are thought to be radiosensitive, and laser therapy may be effective for obstructive lumenal tumours.

Stenting of a stricture may be possible; e.g. with the endoscopic insertion of an Atkinson-Nottingham tube for carcinoma of the oesophagus. Endoscopic dilatation of tumours is also frequently of benefit. This will probably need to be repeated at intervals.

If it is not possible to relieve the patient's dysphagia by any other means, consideration should be given to the formation of a gastrostomy. This procedure does not always require a laparotomy. Gastrostomy tubes may now be inserted with a combined percutaneous and endoscopic approach. Fine nasogastric tubes are well tolerated by some patients.

The Key Issues

More Facts and Comments

"*Gastrostomy or nasogastric feeding is important to maintain nutrition in a relatively well patient awaiting surgery or radiotherapy. Beware of starting such a nutritional support measure if it is not going to improve the quality of life. Nasogastric feeding in terminal illness can result in the prolongation of life or the prolongation of death. For example, if a patient cannot swallow past a nasogastric tube, they may die continually spitting saliva and in a very severe cachectic state. This may not be viewed as an aesthetic death!*"

J M Leiper, Consultant in Palliative Medicine

How Do You Know If You Have Been Effective?

Review the success, with the patient and carers, of the measures above.

Looking forward

The problem of dysphagia exemplifies how palliative care is all about teamwork. Your assessment of the case is the first step to management, which will require the services of other professionals. Skilled nursing is important, to ensure adequate oral hygiene and hydration, correct positioning after meals and reduced air swallowing.

C6   *The Patient is Nauseated*

The Key Issues	*More Facts and Comments*

What Do You Think About?

Nausea is both upsetting and distressing to the patient. You have to think about the likely cause. In other words, is it due to disease or treatment?

Nausea and vomiting are under the physiological control of the vomiting centre in the medulla. This is in turn under the influence of higher centres in the brain, the vestibular nuclei, the chemoreceptor trigger zone in the floor of the fourth ventricle and abdominal organs.

Causes of nausea are listed below.

- Toxic - metabolic conditions, such as uraemia, **hypercalcaemia** and septicaemia.
- Drugs - **opioids**, antibiotics, chemotherapeutic agents, digoxin, carbamazepine, theophylline and many other drugs.
- Mechanical - reflux, gastric stasis and intestinal obstruction due to recurrent tumour or **constipation.**
- Psychological - anxiety etc.
- Raised intracranial pressure.

❝ Nausea and vomiting due to morphine therapy is not inevitable. It occurs in about one in three patients. Tolerance develops to nausea and vomiting, and it usually disappears after seven to ten days. In hospice units anti-emetics are no longer given routinely with opioids. ❞
Ray Corcoran, Consultant in Palliative Medicine

The Key Issues	*More Facts and Comments*

What Should You Try To Find Out?

What is the pattern of the nausea? Is it intermittent or persistent? Is it of recent onset?

What is the likely extent of the patient's disease? Does this explain the patient's nausea?

What treatment is the patient receiving?

What Do You Do?

- Review all drug therapy.
- Check blood urea, electrolytes and calcium.
- Examine the patient, including a rectal examination if constipation is suspected.
- Explain the likely cause to the patient.
- Consider simple measures such as dietary advice.

Remember that proximity to a kitchen or food trolley with the attendant smells may precipitate nausea in some susceptible patients.

The nauseated patient will tolerate cool fizzy drinks better than tea, coffee or still drinks. Low-fat foods and savoury foods can be eaten when other sweeter foods are nauseating.

The Key Issues

Prescribe an anti-emetic appropriate to the likely cause of the patient's symptom.

More Facts and Comments

Anti-emetic drugs may be classified into those that act predominantly centrally, on dopaminergic, cholinergic or histamine receptors in the brain, and those that act peripherally.

Metoclopramide and domperidone act predominantly on the upper gastro-intestinal tract, promoting gastric emptying. They are therefore the drugs of choice for reflux and gastric stasis.

Peripherally acting anti-emetics should be avoided in mechanical intestinal obstruction, as they may aggravate symptoms. Cisapride is a newer drug which is thought to promote release of acetylcholine in the gut wall. This drug, while not specifically an anti-emetic, promotes gastric emptying and increases intestinal transit. Other anti-emetic drugs such as haloperidol, prochlorperazine, cyclizine, methotrimeprazine and chlorpromazine all act centrally. In high doses these drugs may therefore be expected to have sedative and other adverse central effects.

Combinations of anti-emetic drugs may be required in some patients. If so, drugs with different modes of action should be used.

Corticosteroids are the drugs of choice for the treatment of symptoms (including nausea and vomiting) due to raised intracranial pressure.

In some patients, when all else has failed and no hypercalcaemia or raised intracranial pressure has been found, dexamethasone, through an unexplained mechanism, will help to control nausea. The starting dose is 16 mg on first day reducing by 4 mg daily to a maintenance dose of 2-6 mg daily.

The Key Issues	*More Facts and Comments*

How Do You Know If You Have Been Effective?

Review the patient. Make sure to explain that nausea associated with opioids is short-lasting, and tolerance will develop in a few days.

Looking forward

No medical measure will be effective unless adequate emotional support is given to both patient and relatives. Nausea that prohibits eating upsets the family more than anything - apart from pain.

C7 *The Patient is Vomiting*

The Key Issues	*More Facts and Comments*

What Do You Think About?

All the conditions that cause nausea may equally result in vomiting.

Although vomiting frequently relieves the sensation of nausea it is distressing and worrying to both the patient and family.

What Should You Try To Find Out?

Take a careful history, establishing the pattern and frequency of the vomiting. Effortless vomiting, with little warning, at the end of a day may suggest gastric outlet obstruction. Forceful or projectile vomiting early in the day, especially if associated with headache, suggests raised intracranial pressure.

A cause additional to those for nausea is cough-induced vomiting. This can simply be helped by controlling the cough.

"*Relatives and those caring for a patient are much more aware of a patient's vomiting than they are of his or her nausea. This may often be quite alarming for them and frequently leads to major anxieties about adequate hydration and nutrition.*"
W M O'Neill, Consultant in Palliative Medicine

The Key Issues

What Do You Do?

Treat any underlying cause appropriately, e.g. steroids for raised intracranial pressure.

Choose anti-emetics appropriate to the cause of the vomiting. Use combination therapy if necessary.

Ensure that the drugs used are being absorbed. Oral drugs may not be appropriate. Rectal or subcutaneous administration may be required.

More Facts and Comments

Treatment of vomiting is essentially the same as treatment of **nausea** and is frequently easier to control. Patients with a persistent subacute intestinal obstruction may continue to vomit once or twice each day and particularly towards the end of the day. Many patients learn to accept and tolerate this if it means avoiding a further operation. It is generally possible to prevent vomiting in these patients, without the use of nasogastric tubes or the aspiration of stomach contents. A small number of patients may, however, prefer the presence of a nasogastric tube if the choice is between that and some vomiting.

Prochlorperazine, cyclizine, chlorpromazine and domperidone are available as suppositories. Prochlorperazine is also available as a buccal preparation. Most anti-emetics may be administered intramuscularly.

Certain anti-emetics can be administered subcutaneously, if necessary using a **syringe driver**, eg haloperidol 2.5-5 mg/24 hours, metoclopramide 30-60 mg/24 hours, cyclizine 100-150 mg/24 hours.

Chemotherapy-induced vomiting often requires IV administration of anti-emetics. Newer anti-emetic drugs such as $5HT_3$ antagonists (e.g. ondansetron) are licensed for use in chemotherapy-induced vomiting.

The Key Issues	*More Facts and Comments*

Consider whether to refer for active treatment of underlying cause, e.g. surgery for intestinal obstruction, or radiotherapy for brain metastases.

Proper explanation to the patient and family is essential.

How Do You Know If You Have Been Effective?

Adequate reassurance to the patient and family are as important as successful treatment. Sometimes a sense of security and empathy is all that is required.

Looking forward

Consider the possibility of alternative cause and alternative treatment.

Once control has been gained, reduce the anti-emetic to a smaller maintenance dose, before attempting to stop the drug.

C8 *The Patient is Constipated*

The Key Issues	More Facts and Comments

What Do You Think About?

Patients with advanced malignancy often suffer some degree of constipation. This symptom, sometimes regarded as unimportant or a 'normal occurrence', makes a patient uncomfortable, causes colicky abdominal pain, **anorexia**, vomiting, anxiety, and in some elderly patients may cause **confusion**. No effort should be spared to identify the cause and alleviate the problem.

In establishing whether a patient is constipated, it is important to compare both the consistency and frequency of their stools with what has been normal for that patient.

There is a wide variation in the normal pattern. It is estimated that a patient with a normal diet will pass an average of 120 g of stool per day. An intestinal transit time of more than five days is abnormal. Discomfort and straining of more than five minutes is abnormal.

"*Many patients with cancer have a previous history of irritable bowel syndrome or diverticulitis and while these conditions will assume less importance in the face of a diagnosis of malignancy they may still contribute to a patient's symptoms***"***
W M O'Neill, Consultant in Palliative Medicine

What Should You Try To Find Out?

What does the patient understand by constipation?

Is the constipation due to medication:
- **opioids?**
- anticholinergic drugs?
- drugs with anticholinergic action, e.g. chlorpromazine, prochlorperazine or tricyclic antidepressants?

Patients taking weak or strong **opioids** almost always develop constipation. Analgesics containing codeine in small doses are equally capable of causing severe constipation. *It is imperative that prophylactic laxatives are prescribed.*

Anticholinergic drugs cause constipation by a direct action on the gut wall, slowing down peristalsis.

Anorexia - C2   Confusion - C14   Opioids - A4, A6, A7 and A11   **Gastro-intestinal Symptoms**

The Key Issues	*More Facts and Comments*
	The need to treat constipation is usually the consequence of a failure in prophylaxis. *C F B Regnard and A Davies (1986)*
Is the patient's diet appropriate and is there scope for change?	
Is the patient's fluid intake appropriate? Is there excessive fluid loss through **vomiting** or **sweating?**	
Is constipation due to relative immobility or weakness?	
Is constipation due to a malignant tumour of the gut?	" *The obvious most serious cause of constipation may be mechanical obstruction due to tumour.* " *W M O'Neill, Consultant in Palliative Medicine*
Does the patient have any contributory metabolic or endocrine problem?	Biochemical abnormalities such as **hypercalcaemia** and hypokalaemia cause constipation. Hypothyroidism and diabetes mellitus are amongst the endocrine abnormalities which may be contributory.

The Key Issues	*More Facts and Comments*

What Do You Do?

Constipation should be anticipated when giving the patient opioids or anticholinergic drugs and should be treated prophylactically.

When opioids are used, the regular administration of a bowel stimulant and a faecal softener is the preferred approach, delivered as
- one preparation containing a stimulant and a softener, e.g. co-danthramer (available in two strengths),
- two preparations, e.g. senna (stimulant) plus lactulose (osmotic laxative).

Discuss the palatibility of the laxatives with the patient.

Despite the taste, lactulose is well tolerated by many patients. It is essential, with lactulose, to ensure a satisfactory fluid intake.

Explain the mode of action to the patient, including the need to adjust the dose depending on response.

The dose of laxative required is the dose necessary to ensure a bowel action. Constipated patients may require a higher dose initially. To avoid diarrhoea, this is later reduced to a smaller maintenance dose.

A rectal examination should always be performed on a patient with troublesome constipation. Inspection of the anus, prior to a rectal examination, may reveal an obvious painful cause of constipation, such as prolapsed haemorrhoids, an anal fissure or perianal infection.

If the rectum is filled with hard faecal masses, do not give a faecal expander. This will only convert a small hard mass into a large soft one, impossible to expel. The appropriate treatment is to try glycerol suppositories in the first instance. If this is insufficient, a phosphate, or arachis oil, enema may be required. The latter should be dripped in slowly overnight, using a 12-18 inch catheter in an effort to get beyond the impacted stool. Occasionally, digital evacuation is required.

The Key Issues	**More Facts and Comments**
	It cannot be stressed strongly enough that rectal examinations must be carried out on all patients to decide on the appropriate treatment required. *D Doyle and T F Benton (1991)*
Give simple dietary advice regarding adequate fluid intake, appropriate diet and sufficient roughage.	In tumours of the bowel that cause a restricted lumen, the stools should be kept as soft as toothpaste. Use laxatives with softening properties, such as docusate sodium 8-12 tablets a day. Maintain adequate fluid intake and avoid non-digestible foods, fruit peel and pith.
Correct any biochemical abnormality.	
Consult with a surgeon whenever necessary.	Surgical intervention is the obvious treatment for mechanical obstruction. Many patients find the prospect of a colostomy or ileostomy unacceptable. This should be taken into account when surgery is considered.
	However, it must be borne in mind that a patient with recurrent malignant disease may have multiple sites of obstruction, which would not be amenable to surgical resection.

The Key Issues	*More Facts and Comments*

How Do You Know If You Have Been Effective?

Looking back

Did you anticipate constipation when you first prescribed opioids? Did you prescribe the proper prophylactic laxative?

Looking forward

Review the response to treatment with the patient and make any necessary adjustments. It is usually possible both to prevent constipation and to correct it.

C9 *The Patient on Opioids Develops Diarrhoea*

The Key Issues	*More Facts and Comments*

What Do You Think About?

The two most likely causes of diarrhoea in a patient on opioids are

- **constipation** with overflow (spurious diarrhoea),
- inappropriate use of laxatives or other drugs which cause diarrhoea.

However, before assuming any cause, ask yourself three questions.

- Does the patient have true or spurious diarrhoea?
- Is the patient on any drugs that cause diarrhoea?

If **constipation** with overflow is suspected, the pattern of the diarrhoea will give a clue to the cause. This may be confirmed by palpation of the abdomen and digital examination of the rectum.

In most cases [diarrhoea] is found to be spurious, hence the aphorism that in terminal care the commonest cause of diarrhoea is constipation!
D Doyle and T F Benton (1991)

Laxatives, antibiotics and magnesium-containing antacids are drugs that are commonly used in patients with advanced cancer and on opioids. All of these drugs may cause diarrhoea.

" *Frequently a patient on opioids presents with constipation and initially requires high doses of laxatives. Once their bowel has been cleared this may rapidly convert them from a state of constipation to diarrhoea.* **"**
W M O'Neill, Consultant in Palliative Medicine

The Key Issues	More Facts and Comments

- Does the patient have some other incidental cause of diarrhoea?

Some other possible causes of diarrhoea are

- radiotherapy to the abdomen or pelvis,
- chemotherapy, particularly with fluorouracil, cisplatin and mitomycin,
- large resections of the jejunum or ileum,
- ileo-colic fistula,
- ulcerative colitis and Crohn's disease,
- steatorrhoea,
- intestinal infection.

What Should You Try To Find Out?

Take a careful history from the patient. Pay particular attention to the nature and consistency of the stools.

Take a full drug history, with particular attention to laxatives, to antibiotics and to antacids containing magnesium salts.

Consider other causes of diarrhoea.
- Is it steatorrhoea or melaena?
- Is there local colonic or rectal pathology?

Spurious diarrhoea, due to faecal impaction, is mainly profuse watery mucoid discharge. Some degree of faecal matter is always present in true diarrhoea.

Remember that cholestyramine, used to treat pruritus resulting from obstructive jaundice, can cause diarrhoea.

The Key Issues	*More Facts and Comments*

Check for hypercalcaemia as a contributing factor.

Carry out an abdominal examination, which may reveal a loaded colon.

A rectal examination is essential, to detect faecal impaction.

"Rectal examination is an important part of assessment for any terminally ill patient with constipation.
J M Leiper, Consultant in Palliative Medicine

What Do You Do?

Treat the cause, if possible. Bear in mind that an enteric infection may be self-limiting.

Opioid drugs are the mainstay for symptomatic management of diarrhoea. If the patient's cancer pain is controlled, and there is no other indication to increase the current dose of centrally acting opioids, loperamide should be added. Loperamide is a synthetic opioid derivative that, in therapeutic doses, is devoid of central effects. The maximum recommended daily dose is 16 mg, but this can be safely increased in severe diarrhoea. In practice, the dose tolerated will be limited by the number of capsules the patient can be expected to swallow.

"Codeine phospate should not be used as an antidiarrhoeal agent in a patient already on morphine.
W M O'Neill, Consultant in Palliative Medicine

The Key Issues	*More Facts and Comments*

Consider the need for an enema or manual evacuation for persistent low impaction. Regular enemas may be the only way to control the situation.

Monitor any causative drugs carefully, particularly laxatives.

Explain the situation properly to the patient and carers.

How Do You Know If You Have Been Effective?

Check that the patient's symptoms are resolving.

Ensure that the patient is, where possible, involved in the use and dosage of any causative drugs, particularly laxatives.

C10 Should You Set Up an IV Infusion on a Patient Who is Dying?

The Key Issues	More Facts and Comments
What Do You Think About? When a patient is dying you have to pause for a while and honestly ask yourself: "What are the indications for intravenous infusion in this situation?"	*We need to determine what the symbolic indications for an IV line are and what allows some patients and families to set the symbolism aside. Is IV fluid used for the dying, in the absence of specific goal-oriented indications, a ritualistic medical last rite without scientific foundation?* *F I Burge, D B King and D Williamson (1990)*
What Should You Try To Find Out? Will there be any benefit? Is the infusion to treat some specific problem? Is it at the request of the patient or family? Is it at the request of other hospital staff?	The symptom most commonly reported in conscious patients who are clinically dehydrated, is a **dry and unpleasant mouth**. The appropriate treatment for this is simple mouth care. Use mouth washes and treat specific conditions. For example, candidiasis can be treated with nystatin suspension or other topical preparations.

The Key Issues

What Do You Do?

Assess the need for IV fluids.

Discuss management with the patient, the family and with those caring for the patient.

More Facts and Comments

Many patients, relatives and staff feel that to give a patient intravenous fluids is to provide adequate nutrition. This, they feel, will sustain the patient and relieve the distress of thirst, fatigue and weakness.

There is little evidence to suggest that giving IV fluids to dying patients accomplishes these aims.

Some patients and relatives feel that, without IV fluids, the patient has been left to die. The appropriate management in this situation is to discuss, openly and honestly, with the patient and relatives any likely benefit from intravenous fluids. Attention should be focused on the need for adequate oral hygiene and mouth care.

Intravenous hydration can be distressing and in a very ill patient some dehydration can actually improve comfort. Urinary output drops so reducing the need for catheterization, and troublesome bronchial secretions lessen. In bowel obstruction gastric secretions are less, so reducing both vomiting frequency and the need for nasogastric suction.
C F B Regnard and A Davies (1986)

The Key Issues	*More Facts and Comments*

How Do You Know If You Have Been Effective?

Review the patient frequently.

The relatives will always want the patient to die in peace. They will prefer to avoid intubation of any kind. IV infusion might require the insertion of an unnecessary urinary catheter or a nasogastric tube, and may even contribute to 'death rattle'. If you can explain this clearly, in most cases, the relatives will agree that an IV infusion is not for the best.

C11   *The Patient Has Lymphoedema*

The Key Issues	*More Facts and Comments*

What Do You Think About?

Think about the possible causes of lymphoedema

- surgery (e.g. mastectomy involving block dissection of the axilla),
- radiotherapy, causing fibrosis,
- pelvic or abdominal masses,
- tumour recurrence.

Lymphoedema is the accumulation of lymph in the subcutaneous tissue, causing thickening and fibrosis. Usually one limb is affected, becoming swollen, heavy, tight and uncomfortable. The limb becomes increasingly immobile and unsightly.

What Should You Try To Find Out?

If the involved limb has been normal for a considerable time following treatment, you should try to find out if the patient has recurrence of the tumour.

Look out for signs of inflammation.

Static lymph makes the limb vulnerable to infection. A small break in the skin provides access to an ideal growth medium.

The Key Issues	*More Facts and Comments*

Find out if the limb has

- fungal infection, e.g. tinea pedis,
- lymphorrhoea (cutaneous leakage of lymph through small cracks),
- ulcers (only occur in the presence of a combined lymphovenous disorder or cutaneous tumour deposits).

What Do You Do?

Help the patient and relatives to understand why the arm or leg is so swollen. Use simple, understandable, words rather than medical jargon.

Advise the patient and relatives to take the following actions.

- Elevate the affected limb when resting. Arms should be raised to shoulder height using pillows. Legs should be up, when sitting, at least level with the hips. The foot of the bed can be raised at night by 2-3 inches.

An illustrated information booklet for patients can be obtained from: Mastectomy Association of Great Britain, 26 Harrison Street, London, WC1H 8JG.

The booklet details treatment and exercise. It also lists suppliers of sleeves, stockings and pumps.

The Key Issues	*More Facts and Comments*

The Key Issues

- Gently exercise the limb 5-10 times, twice a day.
- Take care of cuts, scratches, and insect bites promptly. Clean well and apply an antiseptic cream or solution.
- Be careful when cutting toe or finger nails.
- Dry well between fingers and toes after washing.

Discuss your patient's management with the physiotherapist, who can advise on the possible role of

- massage,
- exercise,
- compression bandaging,
- intermittent compression pump,
- elastic armlets or stockings.

More Facts and Comments

These measures alleviate lymphoedema.

- Compression stockings and sleeves prevent fluid accumulating and give firm support. They must provide enough pressure. That pressure should be graduated, highest at the hand or foot. Some are made to measure but 'off the shelf' sleeves are usually cheaper and equally effective.
- Massage can benefit the patient, through enhancing lymph drainage from the limb. It can be done manually or with an electrical body massager.
- Intermittent pneumatic compression is delivered by an inflatable sleeve connected to a motor-driven air pump. The limb is inserted into the sleeve, which inflates and deflates cyclically. The variety of makes and models ranges from small portable pumps, with a single chamber sleeve, to larger models, with multichamber sleeves, which inflate and deflate sequentially.

The Key Issues	*More Facts and Comments*
	Compression pumps should be used for a total of 4 hours/day for two weeks. They are useful in the initial, intensive, phase of limb reduction, particularly if fibrosis is present.
	Anecdotal experience suggests that the graduated compression sleeves (Lymphapress, Talley) are preferable to the devices that apply an even pressure all along the limb. Diuretics are occasionally indicated in conjunction with the local measures, and corticosteroids may be helpful in the presence of venous or lymphatic congestion, secondary to a pelvic, abdominal or axillary mass. *J Mansi and G W Hanks (1989)*
Treat any inflamed limb promptly by rest, elevation and an antibiotic.	Regnard and Davies (1986) suggest that limb infection should be treated immediately, using phenoxymethylpenicillin 500 mg 6-hourly or erythromycin 500 mg 6-hourly for one week, then continuing on half this dose for at least six weeks.
	For patients who have repeated episodes of infection, Twycross and Lack (1990) suggest that long-term prophylactic phenoxymethylpenicillin (500 mg daily for one year) is the best way of preventing recurrent attacks and minimising infection-induced fibrosis.

The Key Issues

Avoid
- giving injections into, or taking blood samples from, the lymphoedematous limb;
- blood pressure measurements on the swollen arm.

How Do You Know If You Have Been Effective?

Have you sought the appropriate help? Physiotherapy colleages are only too pleased to help in the management of lymphoedema.

Looking forward

Studying the pathology and treatment of this particular patient will help you anticipate similar developments in others.

More Facts and Comments

More information on lymphoedema in the cancer patient is available in:
Badger C and Twycross R (1988) 'Management of Lymphoedema'. Available from the Study Centre, Sir Michael Sobell House, Churchill Hospital, Headington, Oxford OX3 7LJ.

C12   *The Patient Has a Fungating Breast Lesion With Foul Odour: Dressing Changes Cause Pain and Bleeding*

The Key Issues	More Facts and Comments

What Do You Think About?

Think about the distress the odour is causing to the patient and to her relatives.

Fungating tumours provide an excellent culture medium for bacterial colonisation. This is helped by the debris of dead malignant cells, the meagre blood supply and the compromised immune response. Foul-smelling odours are always associated with anaerobic bacteria.

Even when skilled nursing is provided for the patient with a fungating tumour, she will be distressed by any odour because of her embarrassment and its ability to isolate her even further from relatives and friends. Denying the existence of a bad smell will never comfort a patient acutely aware of it! In time, some patients, but not their relatives, may become less aware of the smell.
D Doyle and T F Benton (1991)

Think also about the distress that bleeding at a dressing change can cause to the patient, family, and even nursing colleagues. This is particularly distressing when coupled with pain, which adds to the patient's suffering and makes a change of dressing an unpleasant experience.

An attempt at removing an adherent dressing will almost always result in damage to the superficial blood vessels. Bleeding can be profuse if a big vessel is involved. Changing an adherent dressing can also be associated with variable degrees of pain.

The Key Issues	*More Facts and Comments*

What Should You Try To Find Out?

Has the patient already had the available specific treatment for the breast carcinoma - radiotherapy, hormone therapy, and cytotoxic chemotherapy?

The visible marker of a disease that literally cuts through to the body surface requires the most sensitive and tactful nursing.

Has surgery, particularly toilet mastectomy, been considered?

Containment of smell, exudate and bleeding must be your primary goal of treatment.

Has **palliative radiotherapy** been considered?

What Do You Do?

Foul odour
Consider measures that may help reduce the odour.

Palliative radiotherapy can dramatically cause shrinkage and occasional healing of a tumour and must always be considered.

Administer systemic metronidazole 400 mg 8-hourly or metronidazole gel topically. Hydrogen peroxide (3%) topically may also help.

An activated charcoal cloth dressing placed over the routine dressings can help remove some of the odour.

A well ventilated environment is often helpful.

Attempts to mask a smell with other odours, e.g. air freshener and perfumes, will fail. The patient comes to associate the new odour with the unpleasant one, and soon it too becomes intolerable... Isolating the odour may be possible using adsorbants such as charcoal ...
C F B Regnard and A Davies (1986)

The Key Issues	More Facts and Comments

Bleeding

A swab soaked in sodium nitrate (1:1000) or adrenaline (1:1000) can help reduce bleeding as can calcium alginate dressings (e.g. Kaltostat).

Pain on dressing change

Consider

- using bismuth iodoform paste - this dressing only needs be changed every three days.
- giving the patient an analgesic half an hour before changing the dressing.

Painful dressing changes should be anticipated and adequate analgesia given before starting.

The dose required for dressing changes will depend on any analgesia the patient is already taking. For patients not already on analgesia, dextromoramide 5 mg or 10 mg sublingually is reasonable. Otherwise, it should be the equivalent of an additional four-hourly dose, e.g. morphine 20 mg in a patient on 60 mg sustained-release morphine twice daily.

Consult

Discuss the problem with the radiation oncologist.

The Key Issues	More Facts and Comments

How Do You Know If You Have Been Effective?

To what extent have you, and your team, been successful in controlling the malodour?

Containment of smell, exudate and bleeding are the markers of successful therapy.

Looking back

It is important to take care in explaining the situation to the patient, but have you been sensitive about the patient's body image?

Looking forward

It is very important to remember that the quality of the patient's life must be preserved at all times.

C13　*The Patient Becomes Immobile*

The Key Issues	More Facts and Comments

What Do You Think About?

Increasing weakness is the most common symptom suffered by a patient with advancing cancer.

This increasing weakness could be the cause of the patient's immobility. If so, it would be of gradual onset. If your patient's immobility developed more rapidly, other causes should be considered.

What Should You Try To Find Out?

Is there a neurological cause?

Does the patient's immobility result from a proximal myopathy caused by the cancer or by steroids?

"*Doctor, he has gone off his legs!***"**
An Alarmed Wife

Impending spinal cord compression, due to metastatic carcinoma, may manifest as: low back pain, sensory impairment or deficit, retention of urine and leg weakness. This is an emergency situation. Advice should be sought immediately from a neurosurgeon, or an orthopaedic surgeon, and a radiation oncologist. A delay of 24 hours could mean irreversible spinal cord damage. Meantime, start the patient on dexamethasone, 16 mg daily.

The Key Issues	*More Facts and Comments*

Has the patient sustained a fracture, possibly a pathological fracture, say, of the femur? It may not cause a lot of pain at rest, but the patient will be unable to bear weight on the leg affected.

Do not hesitate to consult an orthopaedic surgeon. Orthopaedic surgery has much to offer, in fixation of pathological fractures of long bones and in stabilisation of the vertebral column affected by metastatic spread.

Possible factors to consider include
- is the patient becoming anaemic?
- is he or she depressed?
- is the patient over-sedated?

What Do You Do?

Following up the possible causes of the patient's immobility will help you decide the appropriate treatment, if any.

If the immobility simply results from the weakness that often accompanies advancing disease, consider physiotherapy. It can help significantly, by teaching the patient to move within his or her capabilities. More importantly, the physiotherapist maintains hope by maximising movement.

If available, a hydrotherapy pool may enable the patient to experience some movements in limbs normally too heavy to move. This experience, psychologically, can be very beneficial.

The Key Issues	More Facts and Comments

How Do You Know If You Have Been Effective?

Did you exclude every possible treatable cause of the patient's immobility?

If there is no treatable cause of immobility, have you explained this honestly to the patient and family?

Have you asked for the physiotherapist's advice?

C14   *The Patient is Confused*

The Key Issues	More Facts and Comments

What Do You Think About?

Think about the distress this is causing to the patient, to his or her relatives, to other patients and to you and your colleagues in the ward.

Families may carry disturbing memories of their confused relative with them into bereavement. This may influence their ability to cope with life and loss in the future.

The period approaching death can be a time of growth and reconciliation for the patient and the family, a time of healing rifts and saying good-bye. If the dying person is confused, this time may lose its meaning. It can become instead a time of great anguish and distress, not only for the patient but also for the family and those involved in care.

Emotional distress can be enough to cause confusion in some patients. In patients who are dying the reality may be too painful and they withdraw inside themselves in response.
M Murphy (1990)

What Should You Try To Find Out?

It is important, in such a challenging situation, to find out if the patient is really confused or perhaps extremely anxious.

There are many possible causes of confusion.
- Is it due to **uncontrolled pain?**
- Is it due to **constipation**, especially in the elderly?
- Is it precipitated by a metabolic disturbance, such as **hypercalcaemia**, uraemia or hypoxia?

A confused patient may have many underlying reasons to explain his or her state. Some of these causes may be reversible, allowing a restoration of mental lucidity.

Determining the patient's previous mental state and what may be causing confusion will help clarify the hopes and aims of treatment. Without this understanding, it is not possible for a team of carers to manage the problem effectively or to help the patient's family.

Often, the family will be able to provide the most accurate account of the patient's recent mental state.

The Key Issues	*More Facts and Comments*

- Does the patient have cerebral metastases?
- Is the confusion perhaps a manifestation of his or her known cerebro-vascular disease?
- Could the confusion be drug induced, e.g. by psychotropic drugs?
- Conversely, is the confusion due to drug withdrawal, e.g. alcohol, a benzodiazepine or a strong opioid?
- Has the confusion been precipitated by a change in environment, e.g. admission to your ward or transfer from one ward to another?

What Do You Do?

Clinical examination is imperative. Investigations may be important in determining the underlying cause. In practice, confusion in patients who are terminally ill is often due to a combination of factors, with some reversible features and some residual deficit in brain function.

Can any identifiable causes of the confusion be alleviated, e.g. provide more effective control of pain?

The Key Issues	**More Facts and Comments**

However, if you find the patient is suffering from hypercalcaemia, should you be treating this? How actively you treat an isolated biochemical abnormality should depend on: the individual patient, the distress the abnormality is causing and whether any further treatment of the cancer is possible.

In certain circumstances you might need to prescribe a **sedative.**

- Benzodiazepines may be given, eg diazepam 5-10 mg orally or by suppository, midazolam 2.5-5 mg 4-hourly by subcutaneous injection or 15-30 mg/24 hours by subcutaneous infusion using a syringe driver.
- Phenothiazines can be used, eg chlorpromazine 25-50 mg three times a day, orally or intramuscularly, methotrimeprazine 25-50 mg 6-hourly orally or intramuscularly, or in a dose of 100-150 mg/24 hours as a subcutaneous infusion.

Although some confused patients clearly have insight and are in a position to be involved in treatment decisions, the majority do not. The caring team and the patient's family must together decide the best treatment options. Sometimes this can involve sedating a patient who is already quite frail, with the known risk that they may then develop a chest infection by virtue of sleep and inactivity.

Don't look upon the use of sedation as a failure in the management of a confused patient. It might be all that you can do to help.
D Doyle and T F Benton (1991)

The Key Issues	*More Facts and Comments*

- Butyrophenones, e.g. haloperidol, are useful when there are associated hallucinations and paranoia. It can be given in a dose of 1.5-5 mg three times a day, orally or intramuscularly, or 2.5-15 mg/24 hours by subcutaneous infusion.

How Do You Know If You Have Been Effective?

When there is pressure from your colleagues and the patient's relatives to do something quickly, it is all too easy to panic over the management of a confused patient. Did you tackle the problem logically? Did you ensure you had identified the cause or causes? Did you consider whether those causes could be alleviated?

Confusion in a dying patient is distressing for relatives. Did you keep them informed at all times? Did you explain why you had to give the patient a sedative drug?

C15   *The Patient is Extremely Restless*

The Key Issues	*More Facts and Comments*

What Do You Think About?

The underlying cause of restlessness may be physical, mental or a combination of both. It is therefore important to establish with the patient whether they can explain their restlessness.

- Is it part of a **confusional state**?
- Is it related to anxiety?
- Is there some other underlying cause?

Causes

Restlessness has many possible causes.

- Pain and discomfort, constipation or urinary retention may precipitate confusion in an ill or elderly patient. This may show up as restlessness.
- Anxiety.
- Drugs may cause **confusion**, e.g. anticholinergic drugs, tricyclic antidepressants, caffeine and hypnotics.
- Some drugs may cause a state of physical restlessness. Antidopaminergic drugs, such as phenothiazines, butyrophenones (e.g. haloperidol), and occasionally metoclopramide, domperidone and tricyclic antidepressants, may cause akathisia. This is a condition of irresistible motor or physical restlessness, in which there is a constant urge to move about and an inability to sit still. It may also be manifest as fidgeting in a patient who is bed- or chair-bound.
- Drug withdrawal, e.g. from benzodiazepines.

Pain may be more difficult to determine in a restless and confused patient. Knowledge of their disease and a history of their pain prior to the restlessness will give many clues. Particular attention should be paid to pressure areas in a bed or chairbound patient.
W M O'Neill, Consultant in Palliative Medicine

The Key Issues	**More Facts and Comments**

What Should You Try To Find Out?

Is the patient able to describe the problem or fears?

Are those caring for the patient able to describe the problem?

Is the patient in any discomfort?

Is the patient on any treatment or drugs which may be causing the restlessness?

What Do You Do?

Attempt to explain any underlying cause to the patient and carers.

Reassure the patient and carers about how you plan to deal with the situation.

Treat any underlying cause.

Abdominal palpation and, if necessary, digital examination of the rectum should allow the diagnosis or exclusion of constipation or urinary retention as a cause of restlessness.

The Key Issues	*More Facts and Comments*
If necessary, prescribe a **sedative**, such as benzodiazepine, a phenothiazine or a butyrophenone.	When a **sedative** is required, benzodiazepines are the drugs of choice. If the patient is able to swallow, diazepam tablets or liquid should be prescribed (2-20 mg daily in a single dose or divided doses). Otherwise, diazepam may be given rectally as suppositories or, if more rapid effect is required, in liquid form, (e.g. Stesolid rectal tubes). Parenteral preparations of diazepam may be injected into the lumen of the rectum using a small syringe (1 ml or 2 ml) without a needle. Diazepam is unreliably absorbed when given intramuscularly but may be administered intravenously. If repeated parenteral administration is required, midazolam 10-60 mg over 24 hours may be given as a subcutaneous infusion. *Antidopaminergic drugs such as phenothiazines or butyrophenones should be used with caution especially in patients already on these drugs as they may be contributory to the patient's state of restlessness.* *W M O'Neill , Consultant in Palliative Medicine*

How Do You Know If You Have Been Effective?

Review the situation with the patient and carers.

C16   *The Patient is Sweating Excessively*

The Key Issues	More Facts and Comments
What Do You Think About? Excessive sweating can be due to many causes, some of which may be related to the disease. Patients are distressed by excessive sweating because of the inevitable discomfort and embarrassment. Some patients may worry about having an infectious disease, in addition to cancer, that might be contracted by relatives.	Sweating may occur in association with anxiety, exercise, physical distress such as pain and nausea or simply as a normal physiological response to a high environmental temperature. It is common in thyrotoxicosis and may also be seen in diabetes mellitus as part of an autonomic neuropathy. Disease involving the hypothalamus or pituitary gland (such as acromegaly) is a rare cause. Fever due to infection or circulating pyrogenic humoral substances may present as sweating. Lymphomas and liver metastatic disease frequently cause unexplained fevers and sweating. Rarely, drugs - including morphine - are causative.
What Should You Try To Find Out? Examination and proper investigations may help establish the cause of excessive sweating.	

The Key Issues	*More Facts and Comments*

What Do You Do?

Try to treat the cause.

Except in the final days of a terminal illness, it is usually worthwhile treating an underlying infection if, by so doing, the patient's comfort is ensured.

Regular use of a non-steroidal anti-inflammatory drug, such as indomethacin (25-50 mg three times daily after meals orally, or 100 mg suppositories twice daily), may help as may prednisolone (10-30 mg daily) or dexamethasone (2-4 mg daily).

Advise the patient to sleep lightly-clad in a cool room and to use cotton rather than nylon nightwear, bed sheets and covers.

Ensure proper nursing and frequent sponging.

Most patients are assisted more by skilled nursing, frequent sponging and appropriate advice about clothing and bedding than by any medical measures.
D Doyle and T F Benton (1991)

How Do You Know If You Have Been Effective?

Reassurance, explanation and skilled nursing are helpful. Most patients put up with the sweating as an acceptable price to pay for freedom from pain, especially when they understand that it has no sinister meaning.

C17 *The Patient is Twitching*

The Key Issues	*More Facts and Comments*

What Do You Think About?

Twitching is a non-specific term used to describe fine dyskinetic or abnormal involuntary movements. Tics, tremors and myoclonic jerks are included in the term twitching.

Twitching should be distinguished from the fasciculations of wasted muscles.

The cause of twitching should be identified and dealt with appropriately. It is troublesome to a conscious patient and causes anxiety to the relatives.

What Should You Try To Find Out?

Are there any obvious metabolic abnormalities which are treatable?

Tics are repetitive stereotyped movements that can be held in check voluntarily, but only at the expense of increasing mental tension.

A tremor is a rhythmic movement of a body part, caused by regular muscle contractions. Postural tremor is a normal physiological variant, which may be exaggerated in anxiety states, thyrotoxicosis and with alcohol. Resting tremor is seen in extrapyramidal disease, including Parkinson's disease and drug-induced Parkinsonism. Intention tremors are seen in brain stem or cerebellar disease.

Myoclonic jerks are rapid shock-like muscle jerks, often repetitive and sometimes rhythmic. They may be caused by drugs, myoclonic epilepsy or metabolic abnormalities.

Metabolic causes include uraemia, hyponatraemia, **hypercalcaemia**, hepatic failure or carbon dioxide narcosis.

The Key Issues

Is the patient on any drugs which may be causative?

More Facts and Comments

Causative drugs are those which decrease seizure threshold. Main ones are: antidopaminergic drugs, phenothiazines, butyrophenones, metoclopramide, domperidone and tricyclic antidepressants.

Rarely, opioids may cause myoclonic jerks. This normally only occurs for two reasons. The dose of opioid has been rapidly increased or a patient's previously normal renal function has deteriorated, resulting in an accumulation of the metabolic products of opioids.

In our experience, myoclonic jerks are a relatively rare side effect of morphine and indicate either that the dose is too high or that it has been increased too quickly.
H J McQuay, D J Gorman and G W Hanks (1989)

Combinations of all the causes may be common in severely ill patients. An obvious example is a patient on increasing doses of morphine for uncontrolled pain, who also requires an anti-emetic such as haloperidol, and who has an obstructive nephropathy from a large pelvic tumour.

The Key Issues	*More Facts and Comments*

What Do You Do?

If possible, reduce the dose of any causative drug.

If appropriate, treat any metabolic cause such as hyponatraemia or hypercalcaemia.

If necessary, prescribe a **benzodiazepine**. Begin with a low dose and increase until there is a response.

Benzodiazepines, e.g. diazepam or midazolam, may help. Their use will be limited by sedative effects on conscious patients.

How Do You Know If You Have Been Effective?

Review the patient daily.

Discuss, in simple terms, the causes with the conscious patient and with relatives.

C18 *The Patient Has Itching*

What Do You Think About?

Pruritus or itching can cause the patient severe distress through loss of sleep, agony, **confusion,** and to say the least, embarrassment. Consider the possible causes.

- Malignant disease
- Hodgkin's disease
- Melanomatosis
- Cutaneous metastatic infiltration
- Obstructive jaundice
- Rectal or vaginal discharge causing perineal irritation
- A coincidental skin disease

Patients with advanced malignancy may also suffer from coincident cutaneous disorders, such as eczema and psoriasis. The diagnosis is usually obvious, clinically.

Cutaneous infestations, such as pediculosis and scabies, should not be forgotten as a common cause of itching.

The patient's social circumstances may indicate the possibility of conditions such as scabies and the diagnosis can be made on careful examination of the patient and by finding the characteristic burrows in the webs of the fingers and toes, or on the hands, feet or genitalia.
W M O'Neill, Consultant in Palliative Medicine

The Key Issues	**More Facts and Comments**

- Allergy.
- Dry skin, particularly in the elderly.
- Drug-induced, e.g. opioids?

What Should You Try To Find Out?

Establish
- the existence of any systemic cause,
- any history of primary skin disease,
- the presence of other causes.

What Do You Do?

Treat the underlying cause.

Review medication, in case that is the partial or main cause.

The Key Issues	**More Facts and Comments**
Consult with colleagues, particularly dermatologist, clinical oncologist, radiation oncologist and surgeon, whenever necessary.	Proper treatment of coincidental skin diseases or skin infestation may require the opinion of an experienced dermatologist. *Skin care is generally considered a nursing task. Even so, there are many occasions when a team approach is of benefit.* *R G Twycross and S A Lack (1990)* The mainstay of treatment for obstructive jaundice is to relieve the primary obstruction - surgically or by the use of a stent, which may be inserted endoscopically or percutaneously.
Treat the itching symptomatically, as appropriate.	Antihistamines are the usual symptomatic treatment for itching. Non-sedative antihistamines are only effective when the itch is associated with histamine wealing, e.g. dermatographism and urticaria. In all other conditions, sedative doses of antihistamines are required. These are effective because of properties related to sedation, rather than primarily as H_1 receptor antagonists. Other sedative drugs, such as diazepam or nitrazepam, will also be effective. Cholestyramine (one sachet 4g twice daily, if the patient can tolerate the taste) and steroids have been used with variable degrees of success in the treatment of itching associated with obstructive jaundice. Cholestyramine is, however, contraindicated in complete biliary obstruction.

The Key Issues	More Facts and Comments

How Do You Know If You Have Been Effective?

Review the patient daily and reassure him or her of your professional help and understanding. Emotional support is important.

Looking back

An attempt to diagnose the cause should always be made, since specific treatments may then be indicated.

Looking forward

Treatment of pruritus may sometimes need the help of other specialists. Skilled nursing may be as important as medical action. Simple measures, such as a cold fan playing on the exposed skin, can also help. Many patients report that sodium bicarbonate washes, as often as desired, are more effective than any other measure.

C19　*The Patient is Chronically Fatigued*

The Key Issues	More Facts and Comments

What Do You Think About?

Perhaps your first thought in this situation should be:

"Is it due to **lack of sleep** or is it unrelieved by adequate sleep?"

It is also possible that the patient may experience chronic fatigue as a result of the disease, treatment, his or her earlier fears and anxiety.

Chronic fatigue may put some strain on relationships between the patient and family, friends or carers.

Pain, diarrhoea, nausea, vomiting or other sources of discomfort may result in loss of sleep, with consequent chronic fatigue.

Anxiety may similarly interfere with the patient's sleep patterns.

Depression may present as chronic fatigue, in the absence of any history of sleeplessness.

Radiotherapy and chemotherapy commonly cause fatigue. The mechanism is not fully understood. It is thought to be related to an increase in basal metabolic rate, together with the metabolic effects of tumour breakdown, in addition to the obvious psychological and emotional reactions to treatment.

Anxiety about advanced disease and fear of impending death may be sufficient to create a fear of sleep in some patients who may feel that they will die in their sleep. W M O'Neill, Consultant in Palliative Medicine

Lack of sleep - C20　Depression - C23

The Key Issues	*More Facts and Comments*

What Should You Try To Find Out?

Is the patient

- getting adequate sleep?
- in any discomfort?
- anxious or depressed?
- fatigued as a result of treatment?

What Do You Do?

Particular attention should first be paid to any physical discomfort that is preventing sleep. *The initial aim should be to ensure that the patient is free of discomfort at night.*

Provide adequate explanation and reassurance for the patient.

Explain the effects of fatigue to the patient and carers.

If a hypnotic is required, temazepam 10-40 mg at night may help.

Prednisolone 10-30 mg or dexamethasone 4 mg in a single morning dose is thought to be of benefit for patients undergoing radiotherapy and suffering fatigue.

The patient's fatigue can often be a source of major stress in close relationships. Adequate time should be allowed for the patient to express feelings and anxieties. Occasionally, an anxiolytic such as diazepam 2-20 mg at night or in divided doses, may be required.

The Key Issues

Suggest to the patient that they conserve energy and pace themselves, by delegating tasks, reducing visitors and making time for relaxation.

Advise the patient about adequate nutrition and fluid intake.

Treat any underlying **depression** with an antidepressant such as amitriptyline, dothiepin or lofepramine.

How Do You Know If You Have Been Effective?

Arrange to see the patient again. Review any anxieties with them and review effects of any treatment offered.

Looking forward

Set realistic, achievable, goals of symptom control. Adopt a 'holistic' approach to patient management. Allow time to sit and have a leisurely chat with the patient. All these, with caring teamwork, are important in helping the patient cope with chronic fatigue.

More Facts and Comments

It should be explained that, if the patient attempts to do too much on one day, he or she will be unduly tired the next day. They should be encouraged to minimise activities that they find tiring, while maintaining as normal a lifestyle as possible.

The Patient is Not Sleeping

The Key Issues	*More Facts and Comments*

What Do You Think About?

Changes in sleep patterns with advancing years are normal. Many older patients find it necessary to sleep for short periods during the day and also sleep less at night. This is something that many individuals find quite acceptable - a problem only arises when they are ill and being cared for by others.

Many patients do, however, have difficulty in sleeping and it does pose major problems for them.

Is the patient suffering from some physical discomfort which prevents sleeping?

Is there an underlying psychological problem?

Causes

Insomnia has four main sources.

- Physical symptoms, such as pain, diarrhoea, urinary incontinence, **nausea, vomiting** or **dyspnoea** may prevent or disrupt sleep.
- Certain drugs, such as steroids, diuretics, caffeine, may lead to insomnia particularly if taken late in the evening.
- Withdrawal of sedative drugs such as benzodiazepines may cause wakefulness.
- Anxiety and depression - where depression is thought to be the cause, particular care should be paid to the pattern of wakefulness.

" Pain resulting in insomnia may cause a lowering of the pain threshold and an increased perception of pain which is one explanation why pain may be a greater problem by night than it is by day. "
W M O'Neill, Consultant in Palliative Medicine

" Fear of going to sleep is not uncommon in adults with advanced cancer. It should be tackled by sensitive exploration of a patient's fear of death or what he or she believes will happen in the dying process. Simply talking over the fears may help. "
J M Leiper, Consultant in Palliative Medicine

The Key Issues	*More Facts and Comments*

What Should You Try To Find Out?

What is the patient's normal sleep pattern?

What is the pattern of sleep disturbance?

Take a careful history from the patient, with particular reference to physical discomfort or psychological disturbance.

What Do You Do?

Treat any underlying physical discomfort.

If a patient presents with severe pain and insomnia, it may be necessary to prescribe both an analgesic and a hypnotic. This will break the cycle of pain, sleeplessness and increasing perception of pain resulting in further sleeplessness. Temazepam (10-40 mg at night) is a useful choice.

"*The use of morphine does not remove the need for a hypnotic as morphine used appropriately for pain does not cause sedation.***"**
J M Leiper, Consultant in Palliative Medicine

Any drugs, e.g. diuretics or steroids, which may interfere with sleep should be administered early in the day.

The Key Issues

Explore any sources of anxiety with the patient, including any fear of dying. It may be necessary to prescribe a benzodiazepine such as diazepam, 2-20 mg daily - either as a single dose at night or, if appropriate, in divided doses.

Assess the patient for clinical depression and treat accordingly.

Provide adequate explanation and advice on sleeping to the patient.

How Do You Know If You Have Been Effective?

Review the patient daily. Make sure that you have explored all the possible causes of insomnia and have dealt with them effectively.

More Facts and Comments

Antidepressant drugs should be used only where **depression** is thought to be the underlying problem. An antidepressant with sedative properties should be chosen. Remember that it may take two to four weeks before a noticeable benefit is achieved.

"Simple measures such as increasing daytime activity, reducing extraneous stimulation at night and ensuring that the patient is sleeping in a comfortable position and in a comfortable bed may be all that is required. "
W M O'Neill, Consultant in Palliative Medicine

C21 *The Patient Has Nightmares*

The Key Issues

What Do You Think About?

Consider what the patient means by nightmares. What is the magnitude of the problem?

It is also important to distinguish between nightmares, night terrors, illusions and hallucinations, and to realise that not all hallucinations are abnormal.

More Facts and Comments

A nightmare is an unpleasant or a frightening dream, occurring during REM (rapid eye movement) or desynchronised sleep.

Night terrors, while common in children, are uncommon in adults. They occur at a different point of the sleep cycle from nightmares and are accompanied by considerable autonomic and motor disturbance.

An illusion is a false perception of a real object or a misinterpretation of an actual stimulus, eg mistaking a nurse for a relative.

A hallucination is a disorder of perception - a visual, auditory, tactile or olfactory sensation in the absence of a corresponding external stimulus. Hallucinations occur either in wakefulness or in the transition between sleep and wakefulness.

Hypnagogic hallucinations occur when falling asleep. Hypnopompic hallucinations occur when waking. Both are normal and usually simple, such as hearing a telephone or doorbell or hearing one's name being called.

The Key Issues	*More Facts and Comments*

What Should You Try To Find Out?

Explore with the patient his or her understanding of the term nightmare. Is he or she describing nightmares or hallucinations?

Listen carefully to the patient's description of the nightmares.

The content of a dream or nightmare may be very significant. It can indicate fears or anxieties, which the patient is unable to express while awake.

Find out the part that drugs may play in the patient's nightmares.

Drugs may interfere with sleep patterns. Anticholinergic drugs, tricyclic antidepressants, alcohol, caffeine and hypnotics may contribute to nightmares. Withdrawal of alcohol or sedatives may do likewise.

What Do You Do?

Explore any anxieties with the patient.

Discontinue causative drugs or adjust the doses.

Prescribe a neuroleptic drug, such as haloperidol (0.5-5 mg at night), when necessary.

For true hallucinations, seek the help of a psychiatrist.

" *Explanations may be all that is required for illusions, hypnagogic and hypnopompic hallucinations, and nightmares. Any anxieties which emerge in discussion with a patient should be explored.* "
W M O'Neill, Consultant in Palliative Medicine

The Key Issues	*More Facts and Comments*

How Do You Know If You Have Been Effective?

Building up a relationship with the patient, based on trust, caring and empathy, will help them to air fears and anxieties. The concerted effort of the team, including the family, to allay these fears and anxieties, should help the patient overcome his or her nightmares.

Looking forward

Are there any particular experiences with this patient that will help you manage this problem in the future?

C22   *The Patient is Dyspnoeic*

What Do You Think About?

Dyspnoea must be one of the worst symptoms anyone can suffer. In advanced cancer, dyspnoea has many possible causes, from which the actual cause must be identified.

The sensation of being unable to breathe adequately will generate tremendous panic, and fear of imminent death from suffocation.

Watching the patient struggling for breath will provoke anxiety and fear in the family.

What Should You Try To Find Out?

History of previous attacks, onset, presence or absence of cough, pleuritic pain and changes in sputum volume and colour are important clues.

Respiratory rate, pulse rate, blood pressure and observing for peripheral or central cyanosis are also important in identifying the cause.

There are five groups of causes for dyspnoea in advanced cancer.

- The cancer itself, e.g. upper airways, or mediastinum
- Pleural effusion, lymphangitis carcinomatosa, lung metastases, atelectasis, hepatomegaly, ascites.
- Debility, e.g. anaemia of chronic disease, pneumonia, pulmonary embolus.
- Treatment, e.g. post-surgery (pneumonectomy), post-irradiation (lung fibrosis), post-chemotherapy (lung fibrosis, cardiomyopathy, myelo-suppression).
- Other conditions, e.g. anxiety, asthma, chronic obstructive airway disease (COAD), congestive cardiac failure or valve disease, motor neurone disease, chest deformity, obesity.

The Key Issues

Is the patient's anxiety the cause or the effect of breathlessness?

What Do You Do?

Explain the situation to the patient in a frank and gentle way.

Reassure the patient of your sympathy, understanding and help.

Attempt to modify the pathological process with drugs
  • antipyretics,
  • antibiotics,
  • corticosteroids (e.g. dexamethasone in a dose of 8-12 mg daily for several days, reducing to 2-4 mg daily thereafter) to decrease oedema around tumour masses.

More Facts and Comments

Nothing can replace the reassurance given by a calmly confident nurse or doctor, sitting by the bedside, and both anxiolytics and opioids will always take second place to such sympathy and understanding.
D Doyle and T F Benton (1991)

In the long-term management of dyspnoea, treatment should aim to alter the underlying pathological problems, as far as possible. Therapies aimed solely at alleviating dyspnoea should be offered alongside specific treatments. That alleviation can be tapered off if the symptom abates, in much the same way that analgesics can be reduced after palliative radiotherapy for pain.

The Key Issues	*More Facts and Comments*
Attempt gradual upward titration of the opioid to help control tachypnoea.	The patient's respiratory drive can be dampened down by the judicious use of opioids. The dose should be titrated up in small (10%) dose increments above the pain threshold, until the sensation of severe dyspnoea is eased. The respiratory rate must be monitored and will fall as the dose of opioid rises.

Suppress paroxysmal cough with nebulised 5 ml of 2% lignocaine.

Warn the patient against taking anything by mouth for one hour afterwards, because of paralysed gag reflex.

Prescribe an anxiolytic drug.

For sustained effect

- oral diazepam, 2-10 mg at night or in divided doses, or
- sublingual lorazepam, 0.5-1 mg, as required.

For panic attacks

- intravenous diazepam, 5-20 mg, or
- rectal diazepam solution, 20 mg, or
- sublingual lorazepam, 0.5-1 mg.

The Key Issues	*More Facts and Comments*

Drain any large pleural effusion.

Attempt non-drug measures
- cold air from a fan or an open window,
- breathing exercises and relaxation therapy,
- oxygen whenever necessary.

Consult with radiotherapist/oncologist for possibility of palliative irradiation, or chemotherapy.

How Do You Know If You Have Been Effective?

Your understanding - of the somatic and psychological background of dyspnoea, of your role and those of other team members - is essential to effective treatment.

Looking forward

Develop the ability to convey your sympathy and understanding to the patient. This is even more important than drugs, particularly when the patient is in panic.

The Key Issues

It is also important that careful assessment should precede any intervention. Treatment should always be the simplest and most effective available that is appropriate for the patient at that time.

More Facts and Comments

You Want to Know the Difference Between Clinical Depression and Acceptable Sadness

The Key Issues	More Facts and Comments

What Do You Think About?

It is understandable that any patient with any illness will feel sad, angry, bitter and may seem quite 'depressed'.

Sadness can be coped with by allowing it to be expressed in a supporting environment. Sadness must be differentiated from clinical depression, which may require specific drug therapy in addition to psychological support.

This may be the key to resolving difficult pain problems and helping those patients who seem to have 'turned their faces to the wall'.

What Should You Try To Find Out?

Perhaps the most important clues to depression are

- Early morning wakening and the patient's mood on wakening. The 'depressed' patient tends to feel dreadful at the beginning of the day. In contrast, the 'sad' patient will tend to feel worse as the day goes on and the reality dawns again.

Doctors and nurses must train themselves to differentiate between 'sadness' and 'depression'. Remember, too, that antidepressants are not 'happy-making drugs'. The injudicious use of an antidepressant may cause unnecessary sedation, constipation, and dry mouth - making the patient feel worse. There is substantial evidence that most depression in advanced disease is 'reactive'. In other words, it is caused by inadequate control of pain and other symptoms.

The biological indicators - such as disturbed sleep, constipation, loss of appetite, weight and libido - can all be direct effects of the illness, as can weakness, weariness, and emotional lability with a tendency to cry more readily than usual.

The presence of organic disease, contributing to the patient's dysthymic state, should always be borne in mind.

The Key Issues	*More Facts and Comments*
	Cerebral metastases, hypercalcaemia or other metabolic disturbances may result in a severe alteration in mood.
	In terminal illness, suicidal ideas are not necessarily an indication of severe depression. They may reflect an understandable wish not to be a burden, or they may be the result of a mistaken assumption that nothing can be done to relieve intolerable pain. As soon as the social situation improves or the pain is brought under control, such patients are in less of a hurry to die. *A Stedeford (1984)*
• The content of what the patient says. Look for indications of low self-esteem and undue guilt. • Impaired concentration, reduced verbal communication and reduced movement. • A history of endogenous depression.	Sadness occurs in short bouts and may be realistically based on the loss of family, independence or life itself. It may have been triggered by planning a will or funeral, saying 'good-bye' or seeking spiritual support. Patients with sadness rather than depression are normally able to express and discuss their sadness in a rational and philosophical way.
	" *I feel I am a burden to my family. I wish I were dead.* **"** *A Patient*
	" *It would be better if I died quickly and got out of the way so that my husband can marry again while he is still young!* **"** *A Patient*

The Key Issues	*More Facts and Comments*

What Do You Do?

Provide plenty of time for **communicating with the patient,** to

- allow the patient to express fears about uncontrolled pain, the effects of drugs, the process of dying and what happens after death;
- identify the patient's unsatisfied needs, wishes and worries about 'uncompleted business';
- identify the real or imagined insensitivity of those around the patient.

Confirm your findings with other members of the team.

Facilitate communication with the family about the patient's worries and sense of guilt.

Seek all available support, e.g. nurse, relatives, hospital chaplain, colleagues of the same religion or country of origin as the patient.

If you take the time to listen, you will frequently find that depression is traceable to concrete life circumstances. To alleviate depression in terminally ill patients, try to

- facilitate communication with family members,
- help minimise financial burdens,
- diminish the impact of severe body image changes,
- sensitise staff to the emotional needs of patients.

The patient will usually benefit from a leisurely chat with a professional more ready to sit and listen than write out a prescription.
D Doyle and T F Benton (1991)

The Key Issues

Make the necessary adjustments to treatment regimen to bring about better symptom control.

Having decided that an antidepressant is indicated, you must choose which one. Remember that it takes between two and four weeks for any antidepressant to show an effect.

Reassess the patient daily.

More Facts and Comments

Which antidepressant?

In some types of pain, tricyclic antidepressants (eg amitriptyline) have a **co-analgesic** effect with opioids. This may be useful in a patient with pain, particularly when taken at night. Any analgesic effect is probably independent of the antidepressant effects.

Dothiepin hydrochloride is a sedative antidepressant and is best given, like the tricyclics, as a single nightly dose.

Flupenthixol is more anxiolytic than antidepressant, and should be given in the morning.

When a response has been obtained, the dose level should be maintained for at least a month. It may then be gradually reduced to a maintenance dose of about half the initial level, provided symptoms do not recur.

The Key Issues	*More Facts and Comments*

When diagnosis is difficult, giving an antidepressant as a 'therapeutic trial' may be of value - if the patient is expected to live long enough to benefit from it.

Consult with a psychiatrist when necessary.

How Do You Know If You Have Been Effective?

It is important to realise that this situation offers a true test of the professional's ability to provide support - personally and through the team, including the family. It is important not to expect an early response to any antidepressant drug. It takes at least two weeks to show effect, and you should review the patient regularly.

Looking forward

The differentiation between sadness and depression is a matter of picking up cues and pointers, as well as allowing patients to express their fears and offering them our sympathetic support. The lesson to be learned from this situation is to use all available resources in a well-planned effort to obtain maximum relief.

Section D - Context of Care

Section D: Context of Care - An Overview

- Alternative medicine
- Spiritual needs
- Hospice care

- The patient wants to go home for a few days
- Relatives caring at home
- Relatives being involved in care
- Financial support
- Wills

- Making hospital more like home
- Dying patients in side rooms

The Key Issues	*More Facts and Comments*

What Do You Think About?

Is something missing from the support your unit is giving? Is the patient really expressing a need for psychological support?

Have you given the impression that no more can be done - even by way of support?

What sort of complementary therapy does the patient have in mind?

What Should You Try To Find Out?

Does adopting complementary treatment involve stopping a clearly beneficial conventional treatment?

Will it be expensive for this patient?

Has the particular complementary therapy any reported risks or side-effects?

Is it of any proven value?

Patients turn from conventional medicine for many reasons. In some places orthodox medicine is unavailable or very expensive. They may have an incurable disease and be clutching at straws or attempting to improve the quality of such life as remains. It may be that because patients pay for alternative medicine its effect is enhanced. Also patients exercise choice in alternative medicine and this may give them a greater feeling of control over their situation.
R Hull, M Ellis and V Sargent (1989)

Complementary therapies

There is a diverse assortment of therapies, from ancient (e.g. acupuncture) to modern (biofeedback). Some offer fundamental curative treatment (naturopathy), while others place more emphasis on symptomatic remedies (homoeopathy). Some shun any artificial aid (nature cure) while others use extensive medicinal intervention (herbalism). Despite their diversity, a common bond unites the complementary therapies. They all attempt, in varying degrees, to recruit the self-healing capacities of the body. They amplify natural recuperative processes and augment the energy upon which the patient's health depends, helping him or her to adapt harmoniously to surroundings.

The Key Issues

More Facts and Comments

All complementary therapies claim to involve the whole patient in his or her physical, psychological, social and spiritual totality.

Recommended reading

Fulder S. The Handbook of Complementary Medicine. London, Coronet Books (Hodder and Stoughton), 1989.

This paperback edition gives a comprehensive guide to alternative medicine. It covers all aspects of complementary medicine - from the scientific to the social and the legal.

What Do You Do?

Find out how the patient views the complementary treatment on offer.

Stress that adopting a complementary (alternative) treatment need not cut off the patient from conventional therapies.

Discuss the value of the patient's current conventional treatment with him or her and the family.

The Key Issues	*More Facts and Comments*

Advise the patient to go to a certified practitioner.

How Do You Know If You Have Been Effective?

Sometimes, the patient's wish to use complementary therapy is just a way of expressing their needs. They may require more explanation and reassurance that you and the team are doing your best for them.

Ask any patient who goes ahead with complementary medicine to see you, or their general practitioner, after therapy. This could be a good learning experience for you.

"I thought I would ask you, doctor, about it, but I'm not going to go after it anyway."
A Patient

The Key Issues	More Facts and Comments

What Do You Think About?

The spiritual aspect of human life may be viewed as an integrating component, holding together the physical, psychological and social aspects. For those nearing the end of life, there is commonly a spiritual need for forgiveness, reconciliation and affirmation of worth.

At this time, you should consider

- is the patient seeking spiritual support?
- is the need not yet clearly articulated, in someone with a lot of fear or agitation?

Offering help and support

A WHO Expert Committee on Palliative Care found that patients have the right to expect that their spiritual experiences will be respected and listened to with attention. The relating of such experiences, and reflection on their meaning, frequently offers a kind of inner healing. When patient and care-giver have a relationship based on mutual respect and trust, there can be a place for the sharing of stories, conversations about the meaning of life and the purpose of suffering, and even participation in religious rituals. A caring relationship that is able to incorporate spiritual aspects has added potential for inner healing. Two premises must be borne in mind,

- Respect of patient's beliefs is imperative. Care-givers do not have to agree with people's beliefs or practices in order to take them seriously. Non-believers can affirm their contribution to a sense of well-being and integrity in others.

- Supportive interventions in this area must be offered in ways that are non-sectarian, non-dogmatic and in keeping with patient's own views of the world.

An altered spiritual integrity often manifests itself in somatic symptoms, especially physical pain, lethargy and **anorexia,** *for which no physiological reasons can be found. It may be identified in discussion with the sufferer, though finding the appropriate words to describe it may be difficult.*
R Hull, M Ellis and V Sargent (1989)

The Key Issues

More Facts and Comments

Recommended reading

World Health Organization. Cancer pain relief and palliative care. Geneva, World Health Organization, 1990 (Technical Report Series No 804).

Neuberger J. Caring for dying people of different faiths. London, Austin Cornish and The Lisa Sainsbury Foundation, 1987.

"*Am I being punished?*

What have I done to deserve this?

What is the point of life and suffering?

What happens when I die?

How can God let this happen?

I am angry at God!

Can I put things right with God?"

Various Patients

| *The Key Issues* | *More Facts and Comments* |

What Should You Try To Find Out?

It is important to find out several things.

- How does the patient describe his or her culture and/or beliefs?
- Does the patient have a spiritual adviser, e.g. priest, rabbi, minister or imam?
- If not, can the Hospital Chaplain help or can another staff member of the same culture or religion help (e.g. a Moslem)?

What Do You Do?

If you feel unable to cope

- say to the patient that you recognise their need to talk about spiritual matters. Say also you will seek help for them from someone who might understand - such as a fellow countryman or a person of the same beliefs.
- do not give false assurances that everything will be all right.

"I am a Christian but I don't go to church!"
A Patient

The Key Issues	*More Facts and Comments*

How Do You Know If You Have Been Effective?

Try to discover whether the need has been addressed, by seeing the patient and family subsequently.

The patient may appear relaxed and more peaceful once the matter is dealt with.

D3   *The Patient Wants to Make a Will in Hospital*

The Key Issues	More Facts and Comments

What Do You Think About?

Patients may wish to make or revise their will in hospital. If the patient brings up this subject, think about:

- What has prompted the decision?

Possible reasons include
- to arrange disposal of their estate,
- to complete unfinished business.

For the dying person there may be need to complete the relationship within himself and with others. He reaches towards this completeness by trying to finish his life tidily, making a will, putting his affairs in order, making confession and making his peace.

- How is it necessary?

If a patient is legally married and intends that his or her estate be left to the spouse, it may not be necessary to make a will.

❝Making a will is not a topic that a doctor should raise with the patient unless there is some very pressing social need such as providing for young children. ❞
J M Leiper, Consultant in Palliative Medicine

The Key Issues	*More Facts and Comments*

What Should You Try To Find Out?

What advice is available in the hospital?

Is there a family solicitor the patient could contact? If not, is the patient aware of the procedure and cost?

Making a will may require two visits by the solicitor depending on the case. The first visit is for taking the instructions and the second is for signing the will. Fees depend on the amount of work and travelling involved.

The essential requirement in making a will is that an executor be appointed. He or she may be a beneficiary of the will. The signature on the will may need to be witnessed by two people who cannot be beneficiaries.

Are the voluntary services of a solicitor available?

What Do You Do?

Regardless of the patient's social and financial status, respect his or her wishes.

One 'gentleman of the road' had nothing to leave but a wrist watch, but felt if he was going to die he should make a will. A very special solicitor spent an hour with him doing all that was necessary. Now, that is an example of what this word 'dignity' is all about.
O M Craig (1991)

Avoid being caught up in family financial disputes.

The Key Issues

Contact the medical social worker.

Consider the need for witnesses.

How Do You Know If You Have Been Effective?

Looking back

Have you noticed any change in the patient's morale after the will was signed?

It is important to realise that helping the patient to complete 'unfinished business' is as important as controlling their pain.

Looking forward

Would you now find it easier to arrange for another patient to make a will in the hospital?

More Facts and Comments

The medical social worker is an important member of the team. His or her role is virtually without limits. The social worker cannot recommend an individual solicitor but can help the patient decide. They can contact a solicitor of the patient's choice, on his or her behalf. They can also investigate the availability of voluntary solicitor services.

Some hospitals do not allow medical and nursing staff to witness a patient's will. If so, there is normally a nominated administrator who will assist.

"*I have done all I intended to do. Now I will just wait and see what happens next. A Patient (who had just made a will in hospital)***"**

D4 *The Relatives Cannot Afford Daily Travel to Visit the Patient*

The Key Issues	More Facts and Comments
What Do You Think About? Is lack of money the true reason for not visiting?	It is not uncommon to find that **relatives** and friends have a fear of hospitals or disease. Perhaps, too, they realise the patient is seriously ill and have a fear of impending death. Many relatives feel embarrassed about admitting such fears. Indeed, they may not have true insight into their own anxieties. Longstanding conflicts and other reasons may also make relatives reluctant to visit. In any of the above situations, relatives may cite lack of finances, which they perceive to be a more acceptable reason for not visiting.
Who can provide help?	Some hospitals have a welfare rights worker. Most hospitals will have a social worker. Either will see and advise the relatives. Increasingly, social workers regard welfare rights as a specialist area of expertise. *In social work we have always to look at the total person - physically, mentally, spiritually, emotionally, the home, work situation, family interaction, hobbies, the marriage, the children. The patients and family sense this and the kind of questions we ask seem to make them feel we are interested in them as people not patients.* O M Craig (1991)
What can the family do?	A particular family member may be able to help, either by organising their own referral to a welfare rights worker or social worker or by harnessing funds or transport directly.

The Key Issues	*More Facts and Comments*

What Should You Try To Find Out?

Meet the family, assess the situation and discuss briefly the difficulties.

Assess the clinical situation. Can the patient be looked after **at home** or in a hospital or **hospice** nearer home?

What Do You Do?

Arrange referral to a social worker.

In the absence of a welfare rights worker or social worker, one can approach various agencies for help.

If family members are on Income Support, or have a very low income, they may apply to the DSS for reimbursement of travel expenses. If they are not, the social worker can arrange for help. There may also be loans available depending on the circumstances.

Some hospitals have a volunteer co-ordinator, who may be able to put the family in touch with a volunteer driver.

Many hospitals have benevolent funds and access to these funds is usually via a social worker.

There are various charitable organisations that may provide a grant towards recurrent travel expenses. In certain circumstances, the Cancer Relief Macmillan Fund may provide a grant.

The Key Issues	*More Facts and Comments*

How Do You Know If You Have Been Effective?

Looking back

To what extent have you managed to sort out the family's problem with visiting?

Looking forward

Are there any more sources, e.g. of financial support, voluntary transport, that may help other families?

D5　How Can You Make the Hospital More Like Home?

The Key Issues	More Facts and Comments
What Do You Think About? To many patients, admission to hospital might mean restriction of normal activity, restriction of space and a rigid system. To the **relatives**, it might mean strict visiting hours and deprivation of freedom to care for their loved ones.	It is important to realise that flexibility of visiting hours, allowing access for family and friends to visit, may be as important to 'homeliness' as the physical environment. *" A cheerful ward atmosphere may be more dependent on the friendliness and attitude of staff rather than on the decoration and furnishings. "* W M O'Neill, Consultant in Palliative Medicine
• How can hospital be made more like home for the patient? • How can it be made more like home for relatives and friends visiting?	
What Should You Try To Find Out? What simple measures can be taken to improve the decorations and furnishings? What arrangements can be made for the patient's belongings to be brought in to the hospital?	Posters and pictures can brighten up an otherwise dull room. When wards are redecorated, choose bright colours for the walls.

The Key Issues	More Facts and Comments

What particular space can be made for a patient and family?

What Do You Do?

Arrange with your nursing colleagues how to make the patient's stay as comfortable and cheerful as possible.

Encourage the patient to get dressed in normal clothes.

Encourage the patient and relatives to express their wishes.

Encourage the patient, if able, to look after himself or herself.

How Do You Know If You Have Been Effective?

Success is when the patient and family behave as they would at home.

Simply give the patient a bed in a corner by a window and ensure the staff are not obsessional in keeping this area 'tidy'. If the area becomes cluttered with belongings, this perhaps is how the patient wishes it to be.

Some families need to be taught how to visit, to behave as they would at home, to sit and read, knit or watch television together.
R G Twycross (1981)

The patient in hospital who is encouraged to provide more self-care for himself experiences an elevation of morale and self-esteem as he comes to regard himself as a functioning and productive person.
L J Hertzberg (1977)

The Key Issues	*More Facts and Comments*

Looking back

Did you have any particular problems in making the ward like home for some patients or families?

Did you discuss these problems with your colleagues in the team?

Did you involve the patient and family in decision making and arrangements, from the time of admission?

Looking forward

What other measures would make staying in hospital feel more like home for future patients?

D6   *The Relative Wishes to Help in the Patient's Care*

The Key Issues	*More Facts and Comments*

What Do You Think About?

Family members need to feel that they are being helpful in some way. This is most often expressed in a wish to provide some practical help to the patient. Consider

- who wishes to provide this help?
- in what way does the relative want to be more involved?

It can be helpful for a family to be involved in the care of the patient in hospital. The patient needs their presence and support. The relatives need to feel involved and able to alleviate the effects of the disease on their loved one.

A relative's wish to be more involved, however, may simply reflect the fact that they have not been given sufficient information about the patient's illness and progress.

To ignore the family of the dying is to ignore the social system that forms the matrix of existence for the dying person.
E M Pattison (1977)

What Should You Try To Find Out?

Establish from the relatives what help it is they wish to offer and how willing they are to help.

The relative's involvement in the patient's care may be limited, e.g. helping provide drinks and food or assisting the patient to eat. It may include more intimate care, such as helping to bathe a patient. Some relatives may find these tasks extremely difficult. It is important not to assume that a patient and relative have had an intimate relationship in the past.

The Key Issues	*More Facts and Comments*

What Do You Do?

Plan, with your nursing colleagues, a strategy for involving the relatives in the care of the hospitalised patient, if feasible, e.g. meal preparation, shaving, bathing.

Saunders (1972) recommends that the family's involvement in care should start at the time of the patient's admission, emphasising their inclusion in all that happens. Relatives should be encouraged to assist in the routine nursing of the patient, doing many of the tasks they would have performed if he or she were still being cared for at home.

Allow the relative to continue to participate in the care of the patient who loses consciousness in the terminal stage.

66 *It is important to ensure that relatives and indeed the patient are not put under pressure by other people's desire that they become more involved.* 99
W M O'Neill, Consultant in Palliative Medicine

Staying close until the end will avoid feelings of guilt during the last days and help in bereavement.
I Lichter (1987)

The Key Issues	*More Facts and Comments*

How Do You Know If You Have Been Effective?

Discuss with nursing colleagues how helpful involvement of the relatives has been.

Explore the feelings of those involved in care.

Looking forward

How, in the future, would you make relatives more effectively involved in the care of a patient?

What Privacy is Needed to Discuss Issues with a Patient Who Has Advanced Cancer?

The Key Issues	More Facts and Comments

What Do You Think About?

The patient has a **right to know**. On this is based a confidence that he or she will be kept adequately informed about condition and treatment.

The right to privacy is central to the whole issue of communication with the patient.

What Should You Try To Find Out?

Is the patient in a single room?

Is there an interviewing room on the ward or is the sister's room available?

What Do You Do?

Choose the most suitable physical environment. Choose your time carefully.

Dying patients have a right to special consideration, but in practice the extent to which the dying are allowed to exercise their rights depends on circumstances and the attitudes of other people.
I Thompson (1979)

If possible, the patient should be taken to a quiet room on the ward. Make arrangements, if you can, that the patient is seen without interruption.

It is not always possible to move the patient in a shared room from his or her bed.

The Key Issues

More Facts and Comments

It is, however, usually possible to anticipate times when other patients are not likely to be in the ward. If not, you or other ward staff can arrange that adjacent patients move to a day room or elsewhere in the ward.

Drawing the curtains around a patient's bed may be sufficient to create an atmosphere of privacy. If there is sufficient activity in other parts of the ward, a quiet conversation may not be overheard.

"*I knew I had cancer because they avoided me for three days and then they took me into a room to talk to me.***"***
A Patient

"*The most important thing is to ensure that the patient feels that you are not hurried and that you are giving them your full attention. These factors may be much more important than the physical environment.***"***
W M O'Neill, Consultant in Palliative Medicine

How Do You Know If You Have Been Effective?

The patient with advanced cancer expects you to be empathic and sympathetic. The patient may realise how busy you are, but still expects you to provide time to discuss his or her illness and progress, to listen carefully to worries, to understand feelings and to respect the confidentiality of the doctor-patient contract. He or she would not like the conversation with you to be overheard and discussed by others. Did you meet the patient's expectations? If you did, then you have been successful.

D8   *You Wonder if a Dying Patient Should be Moved to a Side Room?*

The Key Issues	More Facts and Comments

What Do You Think About?

Is the move to be made because you want the patient and family to have more privacy?

It may be important not to move a patient from an area where they have been for some days or weeks. It is always important to examine the reasons for wanting to transfer a patient to a single room. There are many good reasons for doing this and a number of bad reasons.

It may be much easier for the family and friends visiting a patient if the patient is in a single room. It allows greater privacy for all concerned. It is, however, important to ensure that the patient does not feel isolated, particularly if relatives do not visit frequently.

" *My wife was dying of leukaemia in the hospital. The bathroom was the only place where we could discuss things freely. On the ward people would hear everything you say!* "
A Bereaved Husband

Is it to avoid a confused, agitated or distressed patient causing stress to other patients?

Is it your nursing colleagues' wish, for one reason or another?

What Should You Try To Find Out?

Discuss the situation with the ward sister and nurses. Explore the availability of a side room.

The Key Issues	More Facts and Comments

What Do You Do?

Make sure that

- the patient would not be avoided on ward rounds,
- the conscious patient would not feel isolated,
- the unconscious patient would receive the necessary nursing care.

How Do You Know If You Have Been Effective?

Review the situation with your colleagues.

Explore the feelings of the conscious patient. Ask relatives what they feel.

In general hospital wards it is all too easy for a dying patient in a side room to be avoided on ward rounds. This occasionally indicates an unwillingness or discomfort on the part of ward staff to deal with a patient's death. Providing a side room for the patient may still be appropriate in these circumstances, but it is important to be aware of the underlying reasons.

"*No one should die alone.***"**
J M Leiper, Consultant in Palliative Medicine

D9   *The Patient Wants to Go Home for a Few Days*

The Key Issues	*More Facts and Comments*

What Do You Think About?

When the patient asks to go home for a few days, this is probably because he or she wants to

- see home
- complete some unfinished business
- be with the family and be 'in control'
- reflect on his or her situation and get the illness into perspective.

You should consider how to allay the family's apprehension about care at home.

What Should You Try To Find Out?

It is essential to find out from the patient and the family

- what are the patient's own expectations?
- what is the home like, especially stairs, toilet, telephone, cooking facilities?

" When a patient is discharged with advanced cancer they may be worse physically than on admission. It is a stage of life for taking calculated risks to achieve time at home that may be precious for the patient and family. "
J M Leiper, Consultant in Palliative Medicine

It is easy to imagine how caring at home may look as if it will be difficult. Some family members may express their fears.

" I am not taking him home until he is better! "
A Wife

" ... but I am not a qualified nurse! "
A Wife

The Key Issues	**More Facts and Comments**

- who can offer **support at home?** Is there a spouse, or a son or daughter, a parent, another relative or friend, or no-one?
- what is the age of the carer(s)?
- what general ability (mental and physcial) does each carer have?
- for how much of the day and night is the home carer available?
- what is the carer's perspective on the aims of care?

What Do You Do?

Allow one or two days to plan discharge.

Contact the general practitioner and district nurse, to
- inform them of the patient's knowledge of the disease,
- report the patient's physical abilities and treatment regimes (e.g. syringe driver),
- enquire about available community support.

❝*It is usually in the patient's best interests to return home, even for a few days, if adequate support is available. It enhances the patient's autonomy and therefore his self-esteem.*❞
J M Leiper, Consultant in Palliative Medicine

The Key Issues	*More Facts and Comments*

Check that the ward nursing staff have liaised with the district nurse.

Meet the patient's carers, to
- discuss the aims of discharge,
- inform them of what **support** may be available for them at home,
- inform them of your communication with the general practitioner and support team,
- discuss with them what to do if things go wrong and whom to contact,
- reassure them, and the patient, of your availability.

If possible, keep the bed available for 1-2 days in case of an early return to hospital.

Carers should be reassured that help and support is available for the patient and the family at home. Usually, it is arranged through the general practitioner, the social worker and community nursing staff.

Help and **support at home** also includes aids such as a bath mat, a bath seat, blocks to raise the height of a chair or bed, or a handrail to ease climbing stairs. These may make an enormous difference to a patient's independence. Many aids can be provided by the local social services department or local health authority. Arrangements for their supply differ between districts.

Prior to discharge, advice should also be provided to the patient and relatives on simple means of lifting a patient or helping a patient transfer from bed to chair. Similarly, advice may be provided by a dietitian on appropriate diet or nutrition.

If you encourage care at home for a few days it is a good practice to guarantee re-admission to the same ward. If things go badly wrong reassure everybody, including the general practitioner, of re-admission before the agreed date.
W Finegan, Consultant in Palliative Medicine

The Key Issues	*More Facts and Comments*

How Do You Know If You Have Been Effective?

Review the patient and discuss with him or her and the home carers, separately, the success of the time at home.

Find out if the patient's account matches up with that given by relatives. If it does not, explore why.

Looking forward

Discharging the patient for a few days will help you assess any coping difficulties and the level of support at home. You will be better aware of the situation a patient is returning to, if they later go home permanently.

D10   *The Relatives Want to Take the Patient Home*

The Key Issues	More Facts and Comments

What Do You Think About?

Does the patient share the relatives' desire that he or she goes home?

Is the primary health care support available to make going home feasible?

Could this be purely the relatives dealing with their own guilt?

What Should You Try To Find Out?

What does the patient want? The patient's desire(s) should take priority.

Would satisfying the relatives' wish disrupt a treatment from which the patient would derive a major benefit?

More Facts and Comments

"In taking a patient home to die the patient's views should take precedence. Don't underestimate the capabilities of a motivated family. Try to avoid conflict and 'signing out against medical advice'. Offer re-admission if things go wrong for whatever reason."
J M Leiper, Consultant in Palliative Medicine

"I promised she'd die at home!"
A Husband

"A promise to look after a relative at home until they die may have been made at the beginning of the illness. For many reasons continuing care at home may be impossible, eg paraplegia, coma, etc. It may be possible to 'release' the carer from the promise by discussing care at home with the patient. Alternatively, a joint interview between carer, doctor, and nurse may help achieve this end. A third option is that hospice care may be acceptable to all parties."
J M Leiper, Consultant in Palliative Medicine

The Key Issues	**More Facts and Comments**

What Do You Do?

Before the **patient goes home,** you will need to establish detailed contact with the carers and with local support services.

The support of the health-care team is vital, as is any financial support that may be necessary.

If the patient's condition permits, arrangements may be made for attendance at *a day care unit* on one or more days a week. Day care is now a major part of the hospice service. Palliative care day centres also exist in general hospitals, and are independent of both hospices and hospitals.

These units offer respite for the carer and provide peer group support for the patient. A wide range of creative and social activities are provided, as well as physiotherapy, occupational therapy, hairdressing, chiropody and beauty treatments.

How Do You Know If You Have Been Effective?

The decisions mentioned above are difficult. Other medical and nursing colleagues will find it difficult too. If you share your feelings with them you will soon find out if they feel you have been effective.

❝ *Reassure relatives that their request to take the patient home does not imply they have to make arrangements for care in the community. The general practitioner and primary health care team can be contacted by the hospital in the usual way prior to the patient's leaving hospital.* ❞
W Finegan, Consultant in Palliative Medicine

D11 *You Need to Arrange Support for the Patient and Family at Home*

The Key Issues	More Facts and Comments

What Do You Think About?

In arranging help and **support for a patient and family at home** it is of the utmost importance to think about what is required.

It is also important to be realistic about the support that is available and can be provided.

Do not neglect to consider whether any help offered will be accepted by the patient and family.

What Should You Try To Find Out?

Establish from the patient his or her degree of independence. What help does he or she feel is needed?

Ask the family what help they feel able to provide? What help may be provided by friends?

Find out what services are available locally. Advice should be sought from general practitioners, nursing staff, social workers and occupational therapists.

Support at home
Most of the following support can be arranged in co-operation with the patient's general practitioner.

Nursing
Practical nursing help - with dressings, supervision of medication, bathing and other nursing tasks - can be provided by local district nurses. In some health authority districts, nurses are attached to general practitioners' surgeries. In others, they are based in local health centres or district health authority clinics.

The Key Issues

More Facts and Comments

Most districts now have palliative care nursing teams (Macmillan Nurses or Support Teams). Such home care and support teams are listed in the hospice directory obtainable from the Information Service of St Christopher's Hospice at 51-59 Lawrie Park Road, Sydenham, London SE26 6DZ. They can be contacted by telephone on 081 778 9252 Ext 262/3.

Private practical or nursing help
There are commercial agencies in most areas which are willing to put relatives and patients in touch with domestic help, companions or nurses.

Financial support
Special provision is made within the Disability Living Allowance for those who have a terminal illness. This facility means their claim is processed immediately. For people over 65 years of age Attendance Allowance is available (Form DS1500 available from GPs and social services departments).

Macmillan grants for any reasonable practical necessity would be considered, e.g. telephone installation, paying extra heating bills, washing machines. Forms are available from GPs, social workers and district nurses.

There are various benevolent societies, particularly for ex-servicemen, retired actors and actresses and other groups. One of these may provide financial support for a suitable patient.

The Key Issues	*More Facts and Comments*

Practical help in the home
Practical aid may be provided by a home help employed by the local authority. A referral may be made via the local Social Services Department.

Some health authorities finance Marie Curie nurses to provide night-time or 24-hour home care. Other health authorities provide night sitter services on an intermittent basis to allow respite for carers.

Many churches have a large network of volunteers who are willing to provide help in the patient's home.

Equipment for patient care
A variety of **physical aids** may be obtained.

Day care units
Day care units are now more widely available.

Meals-on-wheels service
This service, normally provided by local authorities, delivers a hot midday meal daily to the home and may be the mainstay of the patient's diet.

Spiritual support
The hospital chaplain may help liaise with the patient's minister or priest.

The Key Issues	*More Facts and Comments*

What Do You Do?

Discuss care at home with the patient's general practitioner.

Arrange, with the general practitioner's co-operation, referral to the appropriate agencies.

Inform the patient and family of these arrangements.

How Do You Know If You Have Been Effective?

The key to a successful arrangement of support at home is to identify the needs of the patient - medical, social, psychological and financial - and the carers. A close liaison with the patient's general practitioner is essential to secure the necessary support. It is through the general practitioner that most of the required support can be arranged and followed up.

Remember that the general practitioner will be in charge of the patient's care at home.

However, from April 1993 for those who have major support needs in the community, the local department of social services will need to be consulted about discharge.

D12   *You are Asked to Arrange Patient's Transfer to a Hospice*

The Key Issues

What Do You Think About?

Are you clear about just why the patient's transfer to a hospice has been requested by your senior colleagues?

- The patient is terminally ill and his or her prognosis is short.

- The patient is unable to return home because of
    - disability
    - lack of support at home.

- The patient has a distressing symptom such as pain or **nausea** and **vomiting**, which you are finding difficult to control. The hospice might be able to help a little more effectively. Then, if the problems were controlled, the patient could return home.

More Facts and Comments

Hospices and hospice care are concerned with the specialised care of patients with severe and progressive disease (mainly advanced cancer). Curative treatment is no longer effective and death is the likely outcome in the short or medium term. Hospice care organisations aim to provide the highest possible standards of medical, nursing, social and spiritual care, with support for a patient's family both during illness and into the bereavement.

❝ *A hospice is not an ideal place for long term care of a patient with, say, an advanced but nevertheless indolent carcinoma and whose prognosis is likely to be many months or longer. The patient who remains in a hospice for a long period is likely to become increasingly distressed by the number of deaths that he sees around him and the number of grieving relatives.* ❞
T F Benton, Consultant in Palliative Medicine

❝ *Most hospices discharge some 25% of their patients home after particular symptoms have been controlled.* ❞
T F Benton, Consultant in Palliative Medicine

The Key Issues

What Should You Try To Find Out?

What does the patient understand by the term hospice? For some, it might be just another hospital; for others, a place which fills them with fear.

Do your patient's relatives know what a hospice is?

What Do You Do?

Explain to the patient and relatives why an opinion is being sought from a hospice physician or a consultant in palliative medicine.

Do not mislead your patient by talking about going to 'convalescent home', or 'a place for rehabilitation'. Do not use vague terms such as 'a very nice nursing home'.

Explain to the patient that a doctor or a nurse from the hospice will visit the patient in hospital before transfer, to discuss any issues he or she may care to raise.

More Facts and Comments

The number of hospice in-patient units has been expanding during the last two

Hospice services 1977-1991 UK and Republic of Ireland*		
Date	**Units**	**Beds**
1977	39	1036
Dec 80	59	1373
Nov 83	83	1770
May 84	87	1842
June 85	95	1897
May 87	121	2299
June 88	125	2340
Jan 90	145	2602
Jan 91	158	2687

* Data from fact sheets, Hospice Information Service at St Christopher's Hospice, 51-59 Lawrie Park Road, Sydenham, London SE26 6DZ.

The Key Issues	**More Facts and Comments**

Arrange an introductory visit to the hospice, if
- the patient is interested, and
- his or her health permits.

How Do You Know If You Have Been Effective?

Did you alleviate any distress your patient showed when the possibility of going to a hospice was first raised?

Looking forward

Try to visit your patient at the hospice, after transfer.

Patients appreciate your visiting them at the hospice more than you can imagine. They do not want to feel like yet another case, passed from one unit to another.

Reading and References

intentionally left blank

Reading List

Symptom Control

1 Doyle D and Benton T F. *Palliative medicine: pain and symptom control (revised edition)*. Edinburgh, St Columba's Hospice, 1991.

> A concise booklet that gives valuable guidelines on pain and symptom control including drug doses and frequency as well as practical tips. It has an appendix on setting up a syringe driver. The price of this booklet is £2 and it can be obtained from:
>
> > St Columba's Hospice, Boswall Road,
> > Edinburgh EH5 3RW
> > Telephone: 031 551 1381.

2 Doyle D, Hanks G W and MacDonald N (eds). *Oxford textbook of palliative medicine*. Oxford, Oxford University Press (in press, scheduled for early 1993).

3 Penson J and Fisher R (eds). *Palliative care for people with cancer*. London, Edward Arnold, 1991.

> This book is originally a guide for nurses on a hospital ward, in a hospice or in the community. It is, however, a useful book that helps any health professional involved with the care of cancer patients to assess, plan, implement and evaluate the care given. The emphasis is on the consideration of all factors that affect the quality of life - physical, emotional, social and spiritual - not only of the patient but also of the family and the carers.

4 Regnard C F B and Davies A. *A guide to symptom relief in advanced cancer (second edition)*. Manchester, Haigh and Hochland, 1986.

> This useful guide deals with management of pain and other distressing symptoms in advanced cancer. The tabulated information and the flow charts used in this booklet enhance a quick and systematic approach to symptom control. This booklet has a section on symptom control in children with cancer and an appendix on prescribing in the last hours and days.

5 Twycross R G and Lack S A. *Therapeutics in terminal cancer (second edition)*. Edinburgh, Churchill Livingstone, 1990.

> This book is written primarily for doctors. It is a practical, quick, reference book for all those involved in the care of cancer patients. The book provides a framework of knowledge on therapeutic approaches to symptom control in advanced cancer. It also contains chapters on oral morphine and the psychosocial issues underlying palliative care.

Communication

1 Buckman R. *I don't know what to say - how to help and support someone who is dying*. London, Papermac, 1988.

2   Porrit L. *Interaction strategies - an introduction for health professionals.* Edinburgh, Churchill Livingstone, 1990.

> This book accepts the challenge of writing about the complex nature of effective communication. The emphasis is on improving communication with patients, clients and colleagues. While not directly focused on situations of advanced cancer, it provides a blend of the art and science of listening, dealing with crisis, problem solving and managing change.

For those who are keen to read more about the nature of the counselling relationship, the following may provide introductory texts.

1   Burnard P. *Counselling skills for health professionals.* London, Chapman & Hall, 1989.

2   Rogers C. *On becoming a person.* London, Constable. 1974.

3   Smith N. *The impact of terminal illness on the family.* Palliative Medicine. 1990, **4**, 127-35.

A good article that reflects the challenging relationship between the health-care professional, the patient and the family.

Bereavement

1   Raphael B. *The anatomy of bereavement.* London, Hutchinson, 1985.

2   Penson J. *Bereavement - a guide for nurses.* London, Harper & Row, 1990.

Hospice and Palliative Care

1   Saunders C (ed). *Hospice and palliative care. An interdisciplinary approach.* London, Edward Arnold, 1990.

> This book provides practical and philosophical reading based on the work of St Christopher's hospice and its Home Care Team. The book stresses the importance of an interdisciplinary approach when facing the physical, social, emotional and spiritual needs of patients nearing the end of their lives.
>
> The chapter by Mary Baines on 'Tackling total pain' is very interesting.
>
> This book is relevant to doctors, nurses, social workers, physiotherapists and other paramedical staff as well as the family or community physician.

2   1991 St Christopher's Hospice. *Directory of hospice services.* London, St Christopher's Hospice, 1991.

> This is an extremely helpful directory. It provides all the information you need about names, telephone numbers and addresses of hospice and palliative care services and organisations providing help and advice to health care professionals, patients and their families, in the UK and the Republic of Ireland. You may obtain a free copy from:
>
> > Hospice Information Service, St Christopher's Hospice,
> >
> > 51-59 Lawrie Park Road, Sydenham, London SE26 6DZ
> >
> > Tel: 081 778 9252 Ext 262/3.

Spiritual and Religious Needs

1   Neuberger J. *Caring for dying people of different faiths.* London, Austin Cornish and The Lisa Sainsbury Foundation, 1987.

> This little book provides considerable insight into the needs and expectations of dying people and their families and friends, which may arise from their religious beliefs and customs. The author provides a brief history and details of the main beliefs held in the world's major religions including those relating particularly to death and dying which must be sensitively considered by the carers.

Complementary Medicine

1   Fulder S. *The handbook of complementary medicine.* London, Coronet Books (Hodder and Stoughton), 1989.

> All you need to know about the scientific, social and legal aspects of complementary (alternative) medicine is provided in this comprehensive, paperback edition.

World Health Organization and Palliative Care

Effective management of pain and symptoms is one of the priorities of the WHO cancer control programme. WHO guidelines on cancer pain relief are now being used in several countries. WHO is also making efforts to convince governments that palliative care should be part of national health policies and cancer programmes. If you are interested, the following two documents cover the subject.

1   World Health Organization. *Palliative cancer care.* Copenhagen, WHO Regional Office for Europe, 1989.

2   World Health Organization. *Cancer pain relief and palliative care.* Geneva, WHO, 1990 (Technical Report Series No 804).

Miscellaneous

If you are interested in keeping abreast of the literature published on the different aspects of palliative care, we recommend the 'Palliative Care Index' published monthly by the Medical Information Service, British Library. The index contains a list of currently published articles selected from professional journals. The articles are arranged into broad categories such as palliative and terminal care, hospices, symptom control, ethical and legal aspects of death, bereavement, nursing and education aspects. An abstract describing the main content of the article and detailed subject and author indexes are provided. From time to time, selected books are listed in a separate section.

References

Albert J S. *The role of orthopaedic surgery in cancer pain.* In: Twycross R G, ed. The Edinburgh Symposium on Pain Control and Medical Education. London, Royal Society of Medicine Services, 1989, 95-8 (RSM International Congress and Syposium Series No 149).

Baines M. *Tackling total pain.* In: Saunders C, ed. Hospice and Palliative Care - An Interdisciplinary Approach. London, Edward Arnold, 1990, 26-38.

Balint M. *The doctor, his patient and the illness revised.* 2nd ed. London, Pitman Medical, 1964.

Buckmann R. *I don't know what to say - how to help and support someone who is dying.* London, Papermac, 1988.

Bunge F I, King D B and Williamson D. *Intravenous fluids and the hospitalised dying: a medical last rite?* Canadian Family Physician, 1990, **36,** 883-886.

Charles-Edwards E. *The nursing care of the dying patient.* Beaconsfield (Bucks), Beaconsfield Publishers, 1983.

Cooperman E M. *Death: help for the terminally ill and their families.* Canadian Medical Association Journal, 1977, **116**, 468-470.

Corcoran R. *The management of pain.* In: Penson J and Fisher R, eds. Palliative Care for People with Cancer. London, Edward Arnold, 1991, 23-53.

Craig O M. *Reflections.* In: Penson J and Fisher R, eds. Palliative Care for People with Cancer. London, Edward Arnold, 1991, 266-275.

Delhaas E M and Brouwers J R B J. *The spinal and epidural administration of opioid analgesics in cancer patients.* In: Twycross R G, ed. The Edinburgh Symposium on Pain Control and Medical Education. London, Royal Society of Medicine Services, 1989, 91-93 (RSM International Congress and Symposium Series No 149).

Doyle D and Benton T F. *Palliative medicine - pain and symptom control.* Edinburgh, St Columba's Hospice, 1991.

References

Finlay I. *The management of other frequently encountered symptoms.* In: Penson J and Fisher R, eds. Palliative Care for People With Cancer. London, Edward Arnold, 1991, 54-76.

Gallagher-Alfred C R. *Nutritional care of the terminally ill patient and family.* In: Penson J and Fisher R, eds. Palliative Care for People with Cancer. London, Edward Arnold, 1991, 91-104.

Halley B J and Hardin K N. *Perceptions of seriously ill patients: does diagnosis make a difference?* Patient Education and Counselling, 1988, **12**, 259-265.

Hanks G W. *The management of cancer pain. Clinical Dialogue.* Staines (Middlesex), Pacemaker Medical Publishing, 1988.

Hanks G W. *Cancer pain - the problem areas.* Cancer Surveys, 1988, **7** (1), 1-4.

Hanks G W. *Oral morphine in cancer pain: fact and fiction.* In: Twycross R G, ed. The Edinburgh Symposium on Pain Control and Medical Education. London, Royal Society of Medicine Services, 1989, 39-46 (RSM International Congress and Symposium Series No 149).

Hanks G W and Twycross R G. *Pain, the physiological antagonist of opioid analgesics.* Lancet, 1984, **i**, 1477-1478.

Hertzberg L J. *Living in a cancer unit.* In: Pattison E M, ed. The Experience of Dying. Englewood Cliffs, N J, Prentice-Hall, 1977.

Hoskin P J and Hanks G W. *The management of symptoms in advanced cancer: experience in a hospital based continuing care unit.* Journal of Royal Society of Medicine, 1988, **81**, 341-344.

Hull R, Ellis M and Sargent V. *Teamwork in palliative care.* Oxford, Radcliffe Medical Press, 1989.

Hunt T. *Ethical issues.* In: Penson J and Fisher R, eds. Palliative Care for People With Cancer. London, Edward Arnold, 1991, 10-19.

Kearney M K. *Experience in a hospice with patients suffering cancer pain.* In: Doyle D, ed. Opioids in the Treatment of Cancer Pain. London, Royal Society of Medicine Services, 1990, 69-74 (RSM International Congress and Symposium Series No 146).

Lasagna I C. *The clinical measurement of pain.* Annals of New York Academy of Science, 1960, **86**, 28-30.

Leiber L et al. *The communication of affection between cancer patients and their spouses.* Psychosomatic Medicine, 1976, **38** (6), 379-389.

Levin S, Berman C, Barnslen G and Bonne B. *The dying patient-attitudes and responses.* South African Medical Journal, 1981, **59**, 21-24.

Lichter J. *Communication in cancer care.* Edinburgh, Churchill Livingstone, 1987.

Maguire P and Faulkner A. *Communication with cancer patients: 1. Handling bad news and difficult questions.* British Medical Journal, 1988, **297**, 907-909.

Mansi J and Hanks G W. *Management of symptoms in advanced cancer.* Update, 1989, **39**, 82-94.

McCaffery M. *Nursing the patient in pain.* London, Harper & Row, 1983.

McQuay H J, Gorman D J and Hanks G W. *A letter to the editor.* British Medical Journal, 1989, **299**, 684.

Melzack R. *The tragedy of needless pain.* Scientific American, 1990, **262**, 27-33.

Murphy M. *Confusion and sedation.* In: Saunders C, ed. Hospice and Palliative Care - An Interdisciplinary Approach. London, Edward Arnold, 1990, 93-101.

Nuttal D. *The early days of grieving.* Beaconsfield (Bucks), Beaconsfield Publications, 1991.

Oken S. *What to tell cancer patients: A study of medical attitudes.* Journal of the American Medical Association, 1961, **175**, 1120-1128.

Oliver D J. *Syringe drivers in palliative care: a review.* Palliative Medicine, 1988, **2**, 21-26.

Parkes C. *Psychological aspects.* In: Saunders C M, The Management of Terminal Disease. London, Edward Arnold, 1978, 44-64.

Pattison E M. *Helping with dying.* In: Pattison E M, ed. The Experience of Dying. Englewood Cliffs, N J, Prentice-Hall, 1977, 316-326.

References

Poorman S. *Human sexuality and nursing practice.* In: Stuart G S and Sudeen S J, eds. Principles and Practice and Psychiatric Nursing, 2nd ed. Missouri, Mosby, 1983, 661-686.

Regnard C F B and Davies A. *A guide to symptom relief in advanced cancer.* Manchester, Haigh and Hochland, 1986.

Regnard C F B, Pashley S and Westrope F. *Anti-emetic/diamorphine mixture compatability in infusion pumps.* British Journal of Pharmaceutical Practice, 1986, **8**, 218-220.

Rutherford M C and Foxley W D. *Awareness of psychological needs.* In: Penson J and Fisher R, eds. Palliative Care for People with Cancer. London, Edward Arnold, 1991, 173-186.

Saunders C. *The care of the dying patient and his family.* Contact (Suppl 38), 1972, 12-18.

Saunders C (ed). *Hospice and palliative care. An interdisciplinary approach.* London, Edward Arnold, 1990.

Silberfarb P M, Philibert D and Levine P M. *Psychological aspects of neoplastic disease: II - Affective and cognitive effects of chemotherapy in cancer patients.* American Journal of Psychiatry, 1980, **137**, 597-601.

Simpson M, Buckman R, Stewart M, Maguire P, Lipkin M, Novac D and Till J. *Doctor-patient communication: The Toronto consensus statement.* British Medical Journal, 1991, **303**, 1385-1387.

Stedeford A. *Facing death - patients, families and professionals.* London, William Heinemann Medical, 1984.

Takeda F. *Preliminary report from Japan on results of field testing of WHO draft interim guidelines for relief of cancer pain.* The Pain Clinic, 1986, **1**, 83-89.

Thompson I. *Dilemmas of dying.* Edinburgh, Edinburgh University Press, 1979.

Twycross R G. *Rehabilitation in terminal cancer patients.* International Rehabilitation Medicine, 1981, **3**, 135-144.

Twycross R G. *The dying patient.* London, Christian Medical Fellowship, 1987.

Twycross R G. *Cancer pain - a global perspective.* In: Twycross R G, ed. The Edinburgh Symposium on Pain Control and Medical Education. London, Royal Society of Medicine Services, 1989, 3-16 (RSM International Congress and Symposium series No 149).

Twycross R G. *The value of a differential diagnosis in the treatment of Cancer pain.* In: Doyle D, ed. Opioids in the Treatment of Cancer Pain. London, Royal Society of Medicine Services, 1990, 1-15 (RSM International Congress and Symposium Series No 146).

Twycross R G and Fairfield S. *Pain in far-advanced cancer.* Pain 1982, **14,** 303-310.

Twycross R G and Lack S A. *Therapeutics in terminal cancer.* London, Pitman, 1984.

Twycross R G and Lack S A. *Oral morphine in advanced cancer.* Beaconsfield (Bucks), Beaconsfield Publishers, 1989.

Twycross R G and Lack S A. *Therapeutics in terminal care.* Edinburgh, Churchill Livingstone, 1990.

Wall P D. *Foreword.* In: Latham J. Pain Control. London, Austen Cornish and the Lisa Sainsbury Foundation, 1987.

Wallace H J and Forti L A. *Psychosocial adjustment of the cancer patient.* In: Proceedings of the American Cancer Society Second National Conference on Human Values and Cancer, Chicago, Illinois, September 1977. New York, American Cancer Society, 1978, 112-117.

Weisman A D. *The realization of death.* New York, Aronson, 1974.

Index

Index

A

	Page
Accepting feelings	179
Activated charcoal dressing	262
Acupuncture	305
Adjuvants	18, 19, 24, 31, 66
After death	206
Agitation	84, 89, 308, 326
Akathisia	271
Alternative medicine	305, 306
Amitriptyline	45, 285
Anaemia	292
Anaerobic bacteria	260
infection	221
Analgesic ladder	31, 62, 66
Analgesics	18, 22, 30, 261, 262, 293
Ananase enzyme	231
Anger	23, 24, 88, 159, 166, 188
Anorexia	189, 243, 308
primary	223
secondary	223
Antacids	248, 249
Anti-emetics	56, 57, 77, 83, 236, 238, 241, 242, 277
Antibiotics	19, 223, 226, 236, 248, 249, 293
erythromycin	258
phenoxymethylpenicillin	258
Anticholinergics	83, 230, 243, 245, 271, 290

	Page
Anticonvulsants	18, 30, 43
Antidepressants	30, 288, 297, 300, 303
in nerve pain	19
Antidiarrhoeal agents	250
Antidopaminergic drugs	271, 273, 277
Antihistamines	230, 281
Antipyretics	293
Antispasmodics	77, 83
Anxiety	16, 47, 88, 107, 225, 236, 243, 267, 271, 274, 276, 283, 286, 288, 290, 291, 292, 293
Anxiolytics	284, 293, 294, 300
Aphthous ulcers	226, 228
Artificial salivas	222, 231
Ascites	292
Aspirin	39
Ataxia	45
Atelectasis	292
Atkinson-Nottingham tube	234
Attendance Allowance	335
Awareness about dying	165

B

	Page
Bad news	108, 121, 131, 152, 167
breaking of	97
over the phone	121
Bad news staircase	103, 112

				Page
Battle fatigue	..	..	..	157
Benevolent funds	..	..	..	316
societies	..	..	..	335
Benzodiazepine	..	..	..	52, 84, 268, 269, 271, 273, 278, 286, 288
Bereavement	..	..	..	267, 322, 338
recent	..	..	..	205
follow up	..	..	..	208
Betamethasone solution	..	..	..	228
Biofeedback	..	..	..	305
Biphosphonates	..	..	..	56
Bismuth iodoform paste	..	..	..	262
Bleeding	..	..	..	260, 261, 263
Blood calcium	..	..	..	237
Blurring of vision	..	..	..	83
Body image	..	..	..	263, 299
Bone metastases	..	..	..	20, 35, 38, 55, 63
Bone pain	..	..	..	18, 24, 30, 34, 38, 50, 64
Bone scan	..	..	..	21, 50, 63
Bowel obstruction	..	..	..	86, 253
Bowel stimulant	..	..	..	245
Brain metastases	..	..	..	242, 268, 298
Breakthrough pain	..	..	..	49, 65, 80, 81
Breast carcinoma	..	..	..	260
Breathless attack	..	..	..	141
Bronchial secretion	..	..	..	83, 253
Butyrophenone	..	..	..	270, 271, 273, 277

C

				Page
Cachexia	..	..	..	189
Calcium alginate dressings	..	..	..	262
Cancer Relief Macmillan Fund	..	..	..	316
Candidiasis	..	..	..	221, 223, 226, 228, 230, 231, 252
Carbamazepine	..	..	..	45, 236
Cardiomyopathy	..	..	..	292
Care at home	..	..	..	69, 328, 336, 337
Carers	..	..	..	24, 50, 223, 235, 251, 267, 272, 273, 283, 329, 330, 331, 332, 333
Cause of pain	..	..	..	11, 14, 63
Cerebral metastases	..	..	..	242, 268, 298
Cerebro-vascular disease	..	..	..	268
Cesspool halitosis	..	..	..	221
Change in disease	..	..	..	109
Changing awareness	..	..	..	140
Chaplain	..	..	..	27, 208
Checking for understanding	..	..	..	103, 113
Chemotherapy	..	..	..	223, 234, 236, 249, 283, 292, 295
Chemotherapy-induced vomiting	..	..	..	241
Chest infection	..	..	..	269
Chlorhexidine gluconate	..	..	..	222
Chlorpromazine	..	..	..	82, 241, 243, 269
Cholestyramine	..	..	..	249, 281

	Page
Cholinergic receptors	238
Cisapride	56, 221, 238
Cisplatin	249
Climate for talking	100
Clinical oncologist	19, 281
Clinical pharmacist	84
Closed communication	127
Closing discussions	104
Co-analgesics	18, 19, 24, 30, 36, 44, 50, 51, 57, 66
Co-danthramer	245
Coeliac plexus block	36, 66, 67
Codeine phosphate	250
Colic	83, 243
Collusion	131, 133
Colostomy	246
Coma	73
Communication issues:	
not telling the patient	116
patient stops talking	159
patient doesn't want the family told ..	126
patient needs to talk	141
patient's use of words	101
premature reassurance	139, 142
preparing patient for bad news ..	102
previous coping	128
right to know	324
talking about death	202
talking about dying	141
talking to relatives	202
talking with patients	97, 200
time to ask questions	204
time to talk	182
Community nurses	69, 330
Community support	329
Complementary medicine	305, 306, 307
Compression bandaging	257
sleeves	256, 257, 258
stockings	257
Confidentiality	100, 212, 325
Confusion	22, 45, 55, 86, 243, 267, 268, 269,270, 271, 279, 326
Conscious level	73, 86
Constipation	11, 48, 52, 223, 236, 237, 243, 244, 245, 247, 250, 267, 272, 297
with overflow	248
Continuing support	130, 135
Continuous analgesia	24, 66
Continuous pain	24, 30, 66
subcutaneous infusion	49, 73, 74, 75, 76, 81
therapy	30
Coping difficulties	331
strategies	163
Corticosteroids	18, 225, 238, 258, 293

	Page
Crohn's disease	249
Crying	178
Crystallisation	82, 85
Cutaneous metastatic infiltration	256, 279
Cyclizine	52, 56, 83, 231, 238, 241
Cytotoxic drugs	226, 261

D

	Page
Day care unit	333, 336
Deafferentation pain	43
Death	210
and the relatives	206
rattle	254
Debility	292
Defence mechanisms	150
Dehydration	190, 230, 253
Delegating work	182
Denial	111, 118, 126, 144, 150, 205
and the team	146, 151
Dental hygiene	222
Dentist	229
Dentures	222, 227, 229
Depression	35, 88, 163, 164, 223, 265, 283, 285, 286, 288, 297, 298, 299, 301
Dermatologist	281

	Page
Dexamethasone	18, 40, 51, 84, 225, 238, 264, 275, 284, 293
Dextromoramide	262
Dextropropoxyphene and paracetamol (co-proxamol)	62
Diabetes mellitus	244, 274
Diamorphine	69, 76, 82, 83, 84
parenteral dose of	77
Diarrhoea	245, 248, 249, 283, 286
Diazepam	82, 269, 273, 278, 281, 284, 288, 294
Diet	221, 224, 234, 237, 244, 330, 336
Dietary advice	246
Dietitian	234, 330
Different views	198
Differing opinions	116
Difficult questions	138
Digital evacuation	245
Digoxin	236
Distancing	119, 157
Distorted expressions	166
Distress	178, 326
Distressing death	207, 214
District nurses	329, 330, 334, 335
Diuretics	230, 231, 258, 286, 287
Diverticulitis	243

				Page
Docusate sodium	..	..	..	246
Domperidone	..	..	..	56, 221, 238, 241, 271, 277
Dopaminergic receptors	..	..	..	238
Dothiepin	..	..	..	285, 300
Dressing changes	..	..	..	260
Drowsiness	..	..	..	55
Drug absorption	..	..	..	29
Dry mouth	..	..	..	45, 227, 230, 231, 232, 233, 234, 252, 202, 267, 270
Dying				
in peace	..	..	..	198
patient	..	..	..	252, 326
Dysaesthesia	..	..	..	43
Dysphagia	..	..	..	73, 86, 233, 234, 235
Dyspnoea	..	..	..	141, 292, 294

E

Eating : emotional problems in	..	..	..	190
Eczema	..	..	..	279
Elastic armlets	..	..	..	257
Endogenous depression	..	..	..	298
Enema	..	..	..	251
arachis oil	..	..	..	245
phosphate	..	..	..	245
Enteric infection	..	..	..	249
Epidural catheter	..	..	..	69
catheter fibrosis	..	..	..	71
opioids	..	..	..	67, 69, 71

				Page
Exhausted families	..	..	..	178
External beam radiotherapy	..	..	..	41

F

Faecal expander	..	..	..	245
softener	..	..	..	245
impaction	..	..	..	245, 249, 250, 251
Family	..	..	..	24, 58, 131, 225
and the team	..	..	..	132
coping	..	..	..	175
grief	..	..	..	131
guilt	..	..	..	133
relationships	..	..	..	174
roles	..	..	..	131
stress	..	..	..	178
Fatigue	..	..	..	159, 283, 284
Fear	..	..	..	24, 88, 272, 283, 286, 288, 290, 291, 292, 299, 315
of addiction	..	..	..	15, 22, 24, 33, 48
of cancer	..	..	..	22
of dying	..	..	..	143
of impending death	..	..	..	17
of opioids	..	..	..	91
of pain	..	..	..	93
of reccurrence	..	..	..	110
of sedation	..	..	..	55
of side-effects	..	..	..	24
Feeding tube	..	..	..	234

		Page
Fever	.. .. ..	274
Financial support	.. .. ..	335
Fluconazole	.. .. ..	228
Fluid intake	.. .. ..	244, 245, 246, 285
loss	.. .. ..	244
Fluorouracil	.. .. ..	249
Flupenthixol	.. .. ..	300
Food aversion	.. .. ..	189
Forgetting information	.. .. ..	102
Foul odour	.. .. ..	260, 261, 262, 263
Frustration	.. .. ..	168
Funeral	.. .. ..	298
Fungal infection	.. .. ..	256
Fungating breast cancer	.. .. ..	20, 260

G

		Page
Gastric carcinoma	.. .. ..	221
outlet obstruction	.. .. ..	240
stasis	.. .. ..	221, 238
Gastrostomy	.. .. ..	234
tube	.. .. ..	234
General practitioner	.. .. ..	204, 307, 329, 330, 333, 334, 335, 337
Giving up	.. .. ..	159, 162
Glaucoma	.. .. ..	45
Glycerol suppository	.. .. ..	245
Going home	.. .. ..	138
Guilt	.. .. ..	168, 178

H

		Page
5-HT3 antagonists	.. .. ..	241
H1 receptor antagonists	.. .. ..	281
Halitosis	.. .. ..	221
Hallucination	.. .. ..	83, 270, 289, 290
Haloperidol	.. .. ..	56, 83, 238, 270, 271, 277, 290
Headaches due to raised intracranial pressure	.. .. ..	18, 50, 51
Health-care team	.. .. ..	333
Healthy denial	.. .. ..	144
Hepatic failure	.. .. ..	276
Hepatomegaly	.. .. ..	18, 292
Herbalism	.. .. ..	305
Histamine receptors	.. .. ..	238
Hodgkin's disease	.. .. ..	279
Holistic approach	.. .. ..	7, 285
Home (see also care at home)	.. .. ..	318, 320, 328, 331, 332, 333
Home visit	.. .. ..	139
Homoeopathy	.. .. ..	305
Honesty	.. .. ..	142, 211
Hope	.. .. ..	103
Hormone therapy	.. .. ..	261
Hospice	.. .. ..	32, 46, 84, 316, 333, 338, 339, 340
directory	.. .. ..	335
Hospital chaplain	.. .. ..	310, 336
Hydration	.. .. ..	240
Hydrocortisone pellets	.. .. ..	228

	Page
Hydrogen peroxide	261
Hydrotherapy	265
Hyoscine	231
butylbromide	83
hydrobromide	83
Hyperaesthesia	43
Hypercalcaemia	55, 56, 223, 230, 236, 238, 244, 267, 269, 276, 298
Hypnagogic hallucinations	289, 290
Hypnotic	56, 271, 284, 287, 290
Hypoaesthesia	43
Hypokalaemia	244
Hyponatraemia	276, 278
Hypothyroidism	244
Hypoxia	267

I

	Page
Ileo-colic fistula	249
Ileostomy	246
Imam	310
Immobility	244, 264, 265, 266
Inadequate pain control	167
Indomethacin	275
Infected teeth	221
Information and the patient	100
Information sheets	152
Informed consent	113, 115

	Page
Infusion set	73, 75, 77, 79, 81, 85
priming	77, 80, 81
Insomnia	44, 283, 286, 287, 288
Intention tremors	276
Intestinal infection	249
obstruction	73, 83, 241, 242, 246
Intravenous fluids	252, 253, 254
Invasive investigations	11
Involving the family	172
the team	128
Irritable bowel syndrome	243
Isolation	150
Itching	279, 281

K

	Page
Ketoprofen	39

L

	Page
Lactulose	245
Laxative	243, 245, 246, 247, 248, 249, 251
Lethargy	45, 308
Listening	98, 108, 186
Liver metastases	54, 274
Local anaesthetics	70
Lofepramine	285
Loperamide	250

	Page
Lorazepam	294
Lung metastases	292
Lymphangitis carcinomatosa	292
Lymphoedema	18, 255, 259
Lymphomas	274
Lymphorrhoea	256

M

Macmillan grants	335
nurses	335
support teams	335
Malnutrition	226
Manual evacuation	251
Marie Curie nurses	336
Massage	257
Mastectomy	255, 256
Meals on wheels	336
Medical certificate	208
Medroxyprogesterone acetate	225
Melanomatosis	279
Metabolic abnormalities	56
Metastases	11, 13, 35, 264
Methotrimeprazine	83, 238, 269
Metoclopramide	56, 83, 221, 238, 241, 271, 277
Metronidazole	221, 261
Miconazole	228, 231
Midazolam	84, 269, 273, 278
Mood mismatches	170

	Page
Morphine	30, 34, 41, 48, 49, 52, 53, 55, 61, 62, 65, 69, 86, 90, 91, 250, 262, 274, 277, 287
'flattened' by	52
nausea and vomiting due to	236
Morphine-6 glucoride (M-6-G)	53, 61
Morphine-responsive pain	52
Motor neurone disease	292
Mouth care	252, 253
infection	221
Multiple pains	18
Muscle relaxants	19
Muscle spasm	18
Myelo-suppression	292
Myoclonic jerks	276
due to opioids	277
Myopathy	264

N

Naloxone	53
Naproxen	39
Nasogastric suction	253
feeding	235
tube	234, 235, 241, 254
Naturopathy	305
Nausea	48, 73, 86, 223, 236, 237, 239, 240, 241, 274, 283, 286, 338

	Page
Nebulised lignocaine	294
Nerve block	36, 52
Nerve compression	18, 43
Nerve damage	43
Nerve damage pain	18, 30, 34, 43, 50
Neurogenic pain	70
Neuroleptics	290
Neurological deficit	44, 233, 264
Neurolytic blocks	67
Neurosurgeon	40, 264
New pain	28, 29, 34
Night terrors	289
Nightmares	289, 290, 291
Nitrazepam	281
Non-verbal communication	133
Non-drug measures	18, 30, 51
Non-opioid analgesic	31
Not feeding	189
Notifying the GP	125
NSAIDS	18, 30, 34, 39, 42, 64
Nursing	260, 261, 275, 334, 338
colleagues	89, 299, 322, 323, 326, 330, 334
Nutrition	253, 285, 330
Nystatin	231
pastilles	228
suspension	228

O

	Page
Obstructive jaundice	249, 279, 281
Occupational therapist	64, 333, 334
Odynophagia	233, 234
Ondansetron	241
Open communication	105, 165, 181
Open questions	101, 111
Opioid-resistant pain	34
Opioid-responsive pains	34
Opioid semi-responsive pains	34, 39
Opioid parenteral schedule	76
Opioids	18, 49, 52, 54, 64, 73, 83, 91, 230, 236, 239, 243, 245, 247, 248, 250, 277, 280, 293, 294, 300
'starting point'	61
by mouth	30
by the clock	30
by the ladder	31
for the individual	32
high doses of	34, 48
psychological dependence (addiction)	23
selective tolerance to	52
side-effects of	52
Oral hygiene	222, 226, 229, 231, 235, 252, 253
infection	226, 230, 231
morphine	30, 32, 76, 77, 86

	Page
Orthopaedic surgeon	40, 264, 265
Osmotic laxative	245
Other patients	212, 216
Oxycel gauze	262

P

	Page
Pain	159, 187, 199, 223, 271, 274, 283, 286, 287, 293, 298,
assessment	11, 13, 24, 27, 29, 88, 93, 187
assessment charts	11, 25, 89
characteristics	11, 35, 44
control	14, 18, 30, 33
diagnosis of	12
drugs in	12
emotional factors in	14
in cancer	11, 24
more than one	11, 18, 63
on movement	63
out of control	28
patient's experience of	25
perception of	15, 88, 286, 287
psychological factors in	14
realistic goals	12, 26, 64
reassessment	24, 27
relief clinic	36, 46, 51, 66, 68, 71, 84
response to opioids	30

	Page
severity	11, 14, 26
somatic	24
subjective experience	14
threshold	14, 286
tolerance	88
Palliative care	27, 308
nursing teams	335
specialist	32
units	66
Palliative radiotherapy	19, 30, 34, 41, 42, 261, 293, 295
hemibody	41
(see also radiotherapy and external beam radiotherapy)	
Pamidronate	56
Paranoia	270
Parenteral diamorphine	86
Parkinsonism	276
Paroxysmal cough	294
Pathological fracture	38, 40, 64, 265
Patient's compliance	24, 28
Pediculosis	279
Peer group support	333
Percutaneous cordotomy	66
lumbar sympathectomy	66
Personal support	158
Phenothiazines	269, 271, 272, 273
Physical aids	336
closeness	194
environment	318, 324

				Page
Physiotherapist	..	..	..	32, 36, 51, 64, 257, 259, 265, 266
Physiotherapy	..	..	..	265
Picking up cues	..	..	..	97
Pleural effusion	..	..	..	292, 295
Pneumatic compression pumps	..	..	..	257, 258
Pneumonia	..	..	..	292
Precipitation	..	..	..	82, 84, 85
Prednisolone	..	..	..	225, 275, 284
Premature reassurance	..	..	..	138, 139
Preparing for loss	..	..	..	209
patients for bad news		..	..	102
Previous coping	..	..	..	128
Priest	..	..	..	310
Primary health-care team	..	..	..	332, 333
Privacy	..	..	..	110, 122, 179, 186, 324, 326
right to	..	..	..	324
Private nursing help	..	..	..	335
Prochlorperazine	..	..	..	82, 238, 241, 243
Prostaglandins	..	..	..	39
Pruritus	..	..	..	249, 279, 282
Psoriasis	..	..	..	279
Psychiatrist	..	..	..	290
Psychological support	..	..	..	299, 305
Psychosomatic experience	..	..	..	24
Psychotropic drugs	..	..	..	268

Q

				Page
Quality of life	..	..	..	162, 263

R

Rabbi	..	..	..	310
Radiation oncologist	..	..	..	263, 264, 281
Radioisotope scan	..	..	..	39
Radiotherapist and clinical oncologist..	..	..	19, 32, 36, 40, 41, 51
Radiotherapy	..	..	..	223, 234, 249, 255, 261, 283, 284
Raised intracranial pressure	..	..	..	236, 238, 240, 241
Reactive depression	..	..	..	297
Realistic goals of pain control	..	..	..	12 26, 64
hope	..	..	..	98, 108
Reassessment	..	..	..	24, 27, 29
Recording conversations	..	..	..	114, 152, 183, 217
Rectal examination	..	..	..	237, 245, 246, 248, 250
Reflux	..	..	..	221, 236, 238
Relatives	..	..	..	110, 148, 163, 172, 186, 187, 253, 254, 299
and breaking bad news	..	..	100
and not telling	..	..	117
anxiety	..	..	187
controlling information	..	..	104
distress	..	..	180
Relaxation in muscle spasm	..	..	..	34, 36

					Page
Renal failure	..	..	..		30, 54, 61
'Rescuer role'	..	..	..		130
Respite for carers	..	..	..		333, 336
Restlessness	..	..	..		84, 86, 271, 272
Right to know	..	..	..		324

S

Sadness	..	..	..		163, 297, 298
Safe environment	..	..	..		170
Scabies	..	..	..		279
Sedatives	..	..	..		52, 55, 56, 84, 269, 270, 273, 281, 286
Seeing the patient after death	..	..	..		207
Senior colleagues	..	..	..		338
attitude to analgesia	..				90
Senna	..	..	..		245
Septicaemia	..	..	..		236
Sexual contact	..	..	..		194
Sexuality	..	..	..		194
Shared room	..	..	..		324, 326, 327
Signs of induration	..	..	..		80
inflammation	..	..	..		80
Single room	..	..	..		324
Skin infestation - pediculosis	..	..	..		279
scabies	..	..	..		279
Skin irritation	..	..	..		81, 82, 83
Sleep pattern	..	..	..		286, 287
Social worker	..	..	..		27, 205, 314, 315, 316, 330, 334

					Page
Solicitor	..	..	..		313, 314
Somatic pain	..	..	..		70
Somatopsychic experience	..	..	..		14
Sore mouth	..	..	..		223, 226, 233, 234
Spinal cord compression	..	..	..		18, 38, 40, 43, 264
Spinal cord damage	..	..	..		43
Spiritual needs	..	..	..		88, 308
care	..	..	..		298, 299, 338
Spondylosis	..	..	..		11
Spurious diarrhoea	..	..	..		249
Sputum	..	..	..		292
Steatorrhoea	..	..	..		249
Steroids	..	..	..		30, 234, 264, 281, 286, 287
Stomatitis	..	..	..		11, 226
post-chemotherapy	..	..	..		228
Stressed relatives	..	..	..		174
Strong opioids	..	..	..		24, 31, 268
Subcutaneous infusion	..	..	..		86, 87, 269, 270
Support	..	..	..		106, 110, 149, 152, 165, 176, 193, 205
at home	..	..	..		329, 330, 334, 337, 338
team	..	..	..		335
Surgeon	..	..	..		32, 246
Surgery	..	..	..		242, 261
Sustained-release morphine	..	..	..		262
Sweating	..	..	..		244, 274

	Page			Page
Syringe driver	73-85, 241, 269	Total pain	14, 24, 28, 37, 50, 88
mixing drugs in	82	physical	14
set rate	78, 81	psychological	14
		social	14
T		spiritual	14
Tachypnoea	294	Touch	180
Talking about death	199	Transfer to a hospice	338
about dying	141	Travel expenses	316
to relatives	202	Treatment not working	107, 136, 185
with patients	97, 199	Tremors	276
Team	15, 58, 110, 115, 116, 155, 158, 172, 175, 191, 200, 267, 269, 291, 295, 299	Tricyclic antidepressants	43, 230, 243, 271, 277
and information	104	amitriptyline	300
senior member of	88	Trust	140
members of	92	Trusting environment	134
ward	91, 92	Truth telling	98
Teamwork	235, 285	Turning one's face to the wall	162
Temazepam	284, 287	Twitching	276
Theophylline	236		
Thinking on your feet	139	**U**	
Thyrotoxicosis	274, 276	Ulcerative colitis	249
Tics	276	Uncertainty	98
Time to ask questions	204	Uncompleted business	299
to talk	182	Uncontrolled pain	267, 277, 299
Tinea pedis	256	Undertaker	208
Toilet mastectomy	261	Unhealthy denial	145
		Unsatisfied needs	299
		Uraemia	55, 223, 236, 267, 276

					Page
Urinary incontinence		..	..	..	286
	retention	..	..	..	45, 271, 272

V

Visceral pain		..	..	..	70
Visiting hours		..	..	..	318
Volunteers		..	..	..	336
	co-ordinator	..	..	..	316
	driver	..	..	..	316
Vomiting		..	..	..	25, 29, 48, 73, 86, 223, 236, 240, 244, 283, 286
	cough induced	..	..	..	240
	due to raised intracranial pressure			..	240

W

Ward		..	..	..	320, 324, 325
	atmosphere	..	..	..	318
Weak opioids		..	..	..	31, 62
Weakness		..	..	..	73, 244, 265, 297
Welfare rights		..	..	..	315
	worker	..	..	..	315, 316
White plaques		..	..	..	226
Will		..	..	..	298, 312, 313, 314

NOTES

NOTES

NOTES